The

RHYTHM
OF MY LIFE

I dedicate this book to the memory of my dear late wife Eileen.

A musician's wife has to be a very special person because she is, in fact, married not only to her husband she is also married to the music world.

The RHYTHM
OF MY LIFE

Have Drums Will Travel

Mike Rubery

BREWIN BOOKS

BREWIN BOOKS
19 Enfield Ind. Estate,
Redditch,
Worcestershire,
B97 6BY
www.brewinbooks.com

Published by Brewin Books 2021

© Mike Rubery 2021

A CIP catalogue record for this book is
available from the British Library.

ISBN: 978-1-85858-742-4

Printed and bound in Great Britain
by Dig Print.

CONTENTS

ACKNOWLEDGMENTS

A special thank you to Judy Gibson for her help and encouragement with this book. I would also like to thank Mr Brian Cox for his help and input.

FOREWORD

Drummers do not always get the thanks and respect they deserve from fellow musicians. In a band room I used to frequent, there was pinned on the wall, a cartoon picture of a happy drummer behind his battery of drums and cymbals. The caption read 'I wanted to be a musician but I became a drummer instead'! This is a story in frequent circulation in the jazz world:

A man goes into a musical instrument shop and an assistant asks, 'Can I help you?' 'No,' said the man, 'I'll just browse round.' Twenty minutes or so later he goes back to the assistant and says, 'I've made my choice, I want one of those and one of those.' 'Oh,' says the assistant, 'you're a drummer aren't you?' 'Yes,' says the man, 'but how did you know?' 'Well Sir, the first thing you chose is a radiator and the second one is a fire extinguisher.' See what I mean!

The truth is very different. Any jazz musician will tell you that the heart and soul of any jazz group, be it a trio or a 16-piece big band, is the rhythm section. And the heartbeat of the rhythm section is the drums. A good drummer can be, and often is, an inspiration to his band. With his steady beat and rhythm, that is Mike Rubery! In this delightful and entertaining book we have, I feel, four sections. The first (Chapters 1-3) is Mike's young life from birth to 21 years. This is a fascinating story of growing up during the war and after, in far from privileged circumstances. The next section (Chapters 4-9) covers Mike's two years National Service and is remarkable for all its adventures, especially his twelve months on Christmas Island just after the Atomic Bomb Testing. The next section (Chapters 10-13) detail Mike's life as a part-time and then full-time pro drummer out on the circuits. It is truly extraordinary, like a *Who's Who* of showbiz in the sixties and seventies. And lastly (Chapters 14-16) Mike's later life as a shopkeeper and a very busy gigging drummer in local Midlands bands, again a *Who's Who* of Midland jazz musicians, then finally the demise of his beloved Eileen. All this is recounted in a style that you will thoroughly enjoy, narrated in crisp flowing sentences and interlaced with many of Mike's hilarious jokes and stories, some of them are actually true! So, what is left to say?

Well, Mike's modesty does not allow him to say so, but I can. He has been, all his life, in such demand because he is an outstandingly excellent, brilliant drummer. He can jazz with the best of them in small groups or drive a big band along with fire and gusto, he can also read music as easily as reading newspaper headlines. A group of jazz musicians discussing a future gig would ask, 'Who's on drums?' and when the reply was 'Mike Rubery' they would all smile with pleasure, for they knew that they would be getting a good drummer and also one who would be super punctual, sober and keep the band (and the audience) squirming with laughter with his inexhaustible supply of jokes and stories, often introduced with an outrageous, 'Now this is an absolutely true story!'

I have not only been privileged to play jazz with Mike, indeed some of our drum and trumpet breaks are amongst my jazz highlights, but he has also become a dear friend. As Mike himself might put it, I can say without fear of contraception that a nicer, kinder man never bit a sandwich!

Now read on, I especially recommend the Preface by J.P. James, another really great guy, who has written from the heart.

Thank you Mike, for everything.

Brian Cox QC

PREFACE

'Offendie' is just a daft name that Mike and I have called each other ever since Mike told me the story about *The Magic Slippers* many years ago. Economic reasons were nudging me to change from being a straight singer into a vocal/comedian and I was still armed with a bag of sheet music just in case an audience did not respond to my sparkling wit. Needless to say 'Offendie Rubery' supplied me with never ending jokes and anecdotes from his vast collection (and still does to this day).

To be honest I feel sorry for people who have never met Mike Rubery, because he is one of the last batch of guys who did his National Service. Those few years played a massive character-building part in Mike's life so, like many men of this period, they became the kind of men you could rely on, they have confidence, self-discipline and are what I call 'hundred percenters'.

As I write this Preface, in September 2020, we seem to be heading towards a second spike of the dreadful Covid-19 corona virus. This awful epidemic paralysed all live entertainment so this book, I believe, is a link to the past. Why spend your precious time reading it? Well, I will tell you. It's packed with genuinely hilarious true stories and it's a social history of a vibrant time in clubland's heyday. There were crazy characters performing their cabaret acts with live backing musicians. Oh yes! No CD backing tracks in those days, you gave your music to the musicians and prayed to God they could play it. There was never any problem in that department if you had Mike Rubery playing for you. Comics would tell jokes that would be frowned upon today, but I must admit they were very funny belly laughs which are very rare to hear today.

Mike's life has been a thrilling ride from a very early age, when he first picked up a pair of drum sticks and he has not put them down since, he lives and breathes drums. Mike's amazing late wife Eileen once said that Mike would die with a pair of drum sticks in his hands, hopefully not for a good few years yet. And so dear reader without further ado it gives me great pleasure to introduce my great mate, my mentor, my best friend 'Offendie Mike Rubery'.

J.P. James (Vocalist/Comedian)

The name 'Rubery' is an old medieval
word which means 'a rough hill'.

Chapter 1

CHILDHOOD

Easter Sunday 28th March 1937, 7.30am was when I first saw the light of day, the day I was born. It was a lovely spring morning and they knew I was going to be a bit of a comedian because my dad looked at my mother and said, 'is this some sort of a joke?'! My dad then said, 'he's a funny looking baby, what are those two warts under his chin?' My mother said, 'you're looking at the wrong end.' I dread to think where Dad put my dummy. Now anyone who knows me will know I put that last bit in just for a laugh, the last thing I want is for this book to be boring, so back to the plot.

We lived in a cottage on Turf Pitts Lane in Canwell, Sutton Coldfield which Mom and Dad rented. It was quite primitive. We had no electricity, no gas and no running water inside the house, the water tap was outside in what we called the wash house. Inside the wash house was a brick-built copper with a small fireplace underneath. Mom would fill the copper with water, then light the fire to boil the water, then she would put the weekly washing in the copper and boil it to get the washing clean. There was a big brown sink, also a cast-iron mangle with wooden rollers and a handwheel that Mom would turn to squeeze the water out of the wet washing. God help you if you caught your fingers in the rollers. No automatic washing machines in those days. My mom kept her saucepans etc in there and Dad also kept his shaving gear in there.

To top it all, the toilet was twenty-five yards away from the house and consisted of a wide plank of wood with a hole cut out in the middle, underneath was an oval shaped bucket which my dad would have to empty a couple or three times a week into the garden, I've got to say we had marvellous garden produce. On the toilet door was a three-inch nail and on the nail were six-inch squares of newspaper, no toilet paper in those days. There was a candle and a box of matches, for night time visits.

We had a large garden, three quarters of an acre of land and Dad was a great gardener, he grew everything you could think of with the help of the bucket. Inside the cottage we had a cast-iron range that my mom would cook on. And what a cook she was, she could cook anything. Our lighting consisted of paraffin lamps and candles, when we went to bed we lit a candle to light our way. So you can see my upbringing was very simple.

But back to my birth. I am an only child and when I was born my mom had a problem, she had a condition called milk fever and was advised not to breastfeed me. My dad worked on the farm four hundred yards away from our cottage and he would bring home the best cream and milk, so I was reared on dairy products.

My dad was born in Hatherton Street in Walsall, Staffordshire on the 15th of April 1908. He was the only child of Alfred and Collette Rubery. My grandmother Collette was married twice, her first husband died leaving her with six children. She eventually met my grandad and they got married when five of Grandma's children were grown up and working, most of them were living away from home. The one son had joined the army, another son worked at the Austin in Northfield in Birmingham. One of the daughters was a lady's maid to the McCorquodales in Wolverhampton. Another son, Clarence, looked after Billy Bunn's Garage in Aldridge near Walsall and Walter was the youngest of the six children, then of course along came my dad who was their half-brother. They moved to William Street in the Butts in Walsall, Walter and my dad attended school which was also situated in the Butts. The First World War was declared in 1914 when my dad was six years old.

I remember my dad telling me that they were so poor at one time, their mother sent Walter to get a loaf of bread and a pennyworth of broken biscuits, she spread mustard on the bread and that was their dinner. On another occasion their mother boiled some cods heads and put them on slices of bread and once again that was their dinner.

Dad told me that during the First World War his sister Mary took him to the cinema to see Charlie Chaplin in a film called *The Bank* and while they were in the cinema there was a Zeppelin raid on Walsall. Eventually the family moved from William Street to Bosty Lane in Aldridge, Walsall. Another story my dad told me was that his sister Gladys went to work at the Streetly Ammunition Works in Bridle Lane, helping the war effort. About this time there was a man with a big black Russian bear which would dance for the local kids when they put pennies in a hat. Sometime later a Zeppelin came over my grandad and grandma's house, it was so low that Grandad said he could hear the men in the Zeppelin's basket talking. A motorcar came up Bosty Lane shining its lights into the sky to direct the Zeppelin towards the Streetly Ammunitions Works but a quick-thinking farmer drove a lorry across the road to stop the car. Dad told me that the man in the car was a traitor and the police arrested the chap with the bear who turned out to be a German spy and inside the bear's wide collar round its neck was a map showing the Streetly Ammunition Works. The good news was the Zeppelin never found the Ammunition Works which was only two and a half miles away.

The family moved from Bosty Lane to a big house near what was at the time Aldridge Airfield and my grandad was the Head Stockman working for a local farmer. In 1918 the First World War came to an end when my dad was 10 years old. After the war three airplanes came to the Airfield, they were like a flying circus run by the aviator Sir Alan Cobham, who was an airman during the war, in the Royal Flying Corp. Sir Alan Cobham and his other two pilots took people up in their airplanes for the princely sum of £1, or £5 to do the loop the loop. My dad used to carry cans of petrol to refuel the planes and on one occasion they put him in the front seat of one of the planes and flew him over Walsall, much to Dad's delight.

The three pilots stayed with my grandparents in the big house and my grandma catered for them for the week they were performing their flying circus. One day they told Grandma to be outside of the house at 11.30am, because they were going to fly over the house. So as instructed she stood outside and the three airplanes came flying upside down at a very low altitude. My grandma ran into the house scared to death, Dad said they were real daredevils. At the end of the week, they left without paying the farmer for the use of the field and nor did they pay Grandma for their board and lodging. My dad's brother Clarence got in touch with someone who asked how much the bill was and he doubled it.

Grandad fell off a bus and cut his face quite badly, he wouldn't go to the doctor, but he did go to work in spite of his injury. While at work the local vet came to treat one of the cows, he asked Grandad what had happened to his face, Grandad told him and the vet gave him some cream. Sure enough his face got better quite quickly. So next time you knock your face about go and see a local vet!

The farm where Grandad worked got sold, so the family moved to Little Hay and my grandad found a job at Shenstone Park Farm near Lichfield. My dad was now 13 years of age and so he applied for a job with his dad at the same farm by lying to the farmer about his age, he told the farmer that he was 14, the age when children left school at that time. He worked from 6 in the morning till 6 at night, 12 hours a day and on Sundays they worked six hours. His wages were 14 shillings a week (70p in today's money).

Eventually Grandad, my dad and his brother Walter ended up working for Mr Walters on a farm on the corner of the London Road and Canwell Drive. It was here that Dad started boxing behind the barn with some of the other workers including another chap who was younger than Dad, who lived in Canwell and also worked at the farm, his name was Joe Robinson. Joe told me he remembered Dad boxing sometimes bare-knuckle.

As my dad got older, the farmer he worked for offered him the job of milk roundsman driving a T-type Ford milk van, he didn't need to ask twice, Dad couldn't wait to get behind the wheel and there were no driving tests in those days. He was delivering milk in and around Four Oaks and Streetly, which was a wealthy area. It was 1934 and this was the year Dad met my mom. Dad delivered milk to my mom's place of work, she was in what they called 'service' working for a wealthy family, Mr and Mrs Leather. Mr Leather was a surgeon and his wife was a hospital matron. They lived in a large house by Sutton Park and had a daughter called Diane who was an Olympic runner. Diane Leather was the first woman to run a mile in under five minutes.

My mom was born in a place called Lovats Buildings, Chadsmoor in Cannock. She was baptised Harriet May but she hated the name Harriet so she always told people that her name was May, her surname was Guy. She had three sisters and four brothers. Her father, my other grandad, was a coal miner and two of her brothers were also coal miners. Her father never drank tea or coffee, he only drank Oxo or beer and was a quiet chap who never said a lot. One of Mom's brothers was a champion darts player called Richard Guy, usually known as Dick Guy, her youngest brother Ron joined the RAF then got married and emigrated to Australia. Mom's eldest brother Alfred had a bad accident in the coal mine and her other brother Jim was a very hard-working man also a coal miner.

Mom's sisters were Gladys who was a wonderful cook, Nell who I thought was quite intelligent and then the youngest sister Elsie, whose husband Walter was a Councillor and was credited for twinning Cannock with a town called Datteln in Germany. My mom was a very good dancer and would attend all the dance halls in Cannock, but her mother would demand that she should be back in the house at a certain time, which she didn't always manage. One night my mom was at a dance and in walked her mother carrying a shopping bag, she sat down and reached into the bag, pulled out a chamber pot and then put it under her seat for everyone to see. The idea of this spectacle was to embarrass my mom into getting home at the stipulated time and as you can imagine my mom could not get out of that place quick enough! After that incident Mom was never late getting home again.

Eventually my mom went into service, as I've already mentioned, and when she was 21 she met this 26 year-old dashing young milkman with the fastest T-type Ford milk van in Streetly. They were married within three months and they lived with Grandma and Grandad Rubery in Little Hay for a short while. Then Dad managed to rent the cottage in Turf Pitts Lane, where I was born, the rent was 7 shillings and 8 pence a week (just under 36p in today's money).

When I was a few months old, Mom and Dad used to take me to Grandma and Grandad Rubery in Little Hay which was the next village to Canwell. The means of transport was my pram, which was pulled by our Airedale dog, he would pull my pram with a lead tied to his collar. Being a strong dog it was no problem, but in fairness my dad was at the other end of the pram pushing and steering. We would go down Camp Lane then cut through the wood into Saw Pitts Lane where my grandparents lived. Sadly, Grandma died in my grandad's arms with heart problems when I was twelve months old, it was a pity I would have dearly loved to have known her. After Grandma died, Grandad came and lived with us. Grandad's name was Alfred and my dad's name was Alfred Cecil Rubery, so to cut out any confusion they called my dad Cecil. However, all his friends called him SOS Rubery.

I was baptised into the Baptist Church, the same as my mother. The gentleman who baptised me was my great-uncle who was a Baptist Minister, he was in fact a very devout Christian, so much so that on a Sunday afternoon he would baptise people in the local river. He would dip people's heads in the river

My mom and dad.

Me aged about 18 months. Look at the size of the drum stick!

and ask, 'Have you found Jesus?' Then onto the next person, 'Have you found Jesus?' On one Sunday afternoon he was performing his baptisms when a drunk came staggering along and my great-uncle grabbed him and dipped his head in the river and said, 'Have you found Jesus?' The drunk said, 'No.' So uncle dipped his head in the river again, 'Have you found Jesus?' The drunk again said, 'No.' So he dipped his head in the river for the third time, 'Have you found Jesus?' The drunk replied, 'Are you sure this is where he fell in?'!

By 1939 the Second World War had started and I was two years old. I had curly blond hair which later turned into dark hair with no curls and now I'm nearly bald. I suppose I could have a couple of rabbits tattooed on my head and they would look like hares from a distance!

During the war we had a few bombs dropped nearby. One such night Mom, Dad and I were in the air raid shelter at the side of the cottage. I used to sleep on the coal house door, Dad had taken it off the coal house and used it as a bunk bed, Mom and Dad slept underneath. There was a big toad who used to be in the shelter and he used to sit on Dad's chest, he was quite tame and Dad got quite attached to him. Grandad would stand outside smoking his pipe, one night Dad said, 'Pop why don't you get in this shelter?' Grandad said, still smoking his pipe, 'if the bomb has got your name on it you will get it.' Well that was okay as far as we were concerned, but what about our neighbours, their name was Mr and Mrs Doodlebug!

That night a bomb dropped just up the road at the crossroads, where Weeford Road crosses Slade Road by the traffic lights, the blast blew Grandad and his pipe into the shelter. The next day Mom and Dad took me in my pushchair to see the bomb crater, I can remember looking down into this big hole and my dad picked up a piece of shrapnel and put it into a handkerchief and gave it to me to hold. I carried it all the way home and I've still got that piece of shrapnel. Dad always said that another bomb was dropped somewhere in the area of Canwell Drive that never exploded, another Canwell man Joe Robinson told me the same story. So if the story is true, somewhere around Canwell Drive is an unexploded bomb…

(I knew a man who fought in the Boer War, the First World War and the Second World War – in fact he couldn't get on with anybody!)

I mentioned that we had an Airedale dog. Well, Dad had some false teeth and I had seen him put them in his mouth. So, one day I found these false teeth lying around and I put them into the dog's mouth just like I'd seen my dad do. I was only a little lad and I thought I was giving the dog a new set of teeth. Guess what, Dad was not happy.

Chapter 2

SCHOOL DAYS

I started school when I was four and a half years of age and attended the Canwell Village School, I don't remember much about that school, just a couple of things. Our classroom was one big room, one half was for the infants and the other half for the juniors. There was an open fire with a guard rail which helped heat the room, we had a long-handled toasting fork, and I remember toasting some bread over the fire.

I remember the girls at playtime would sit on the doorstep and some of the older boys would push the girls backwards in order to see what colour knickers they were wearing. Usually in those days they were wearing those blue bloomers with strong tight elastic around the legs, some of the lads I know have still got the marks on their fingers to this day from the elastic! Of course, at four and a half years of age all this was new to me, I was still learning. One day we were playing soldiers, stamping our feet like soldiers do. The Headmistress's dog used to run around with the kids at playtime and as I was stamping my feet I accidentally stamped on the dog's tail and he bit my leg. The Headmistress who was standing nearby said, 'Oh Michael, shall I put something on that bite?' I said, 'No Miss, I think he likes it as it is.'

My parents tried to do the best for my education so the next school I attended was Hollies Collegiate School which was a private school, it sounds very posh, but really it wasn't. The Headmistress was a lady called Mrs Wood, who I might add was a hard woman, in fact she was fearsome. She would dish out punishment at the drop of a hat (so all hats were confiscated). If she had been in the Gestapo she would have been thrown out for cruelty and I was on the receiving end of her discipline a few times.

It was at this school where I first met a young girl by the name of Brenda Godfrey who became a lifelong friend to this day (I will tell you more about

Brenda later on). I remember the school had some sort of a percussion band and I was given a drum suspended around my neck, plus two drum sticks. I was about six years of age and I loved it. My mother told me that when I was really small, I would march up and down the garden banging a tin tray with a wooden spoon. So, fate was beginning to play its part in forming my life.

After five years my parents decided to take me away from Hollies Collegiate School. To be honest I didn't fit in as I was a slow learner, not at all academic and I did seem to be getting into trouble quite often, mostly for fighting. With my dad being an amateur boxer, he used to teach me to box and he always told me if someone picks on you just give them a good smack on the nose, you might get a good hiding but the chances are you won't and either way they won't bother you again.

So, I found myself at another new school, Hill Boys in Mere Green. Now would you believe on my first day one of the lads started pushing me around during playtime. Being a new boy I didn't want to get into any trouble so to get out of his way I went into the classroom. I was not aware of the school rule that boys were not allowed in the classrooms at playtime unless it was raining. So, I was in the classroom when bully boy followed me in and cornered me up against the wall, that was it as far as I was concerned, enough was enough. I hit him bang right on the nose, which broke, blood all over his face. Just as I hit him, our teacher Mr Taffy Davis walked into the room and saw what had happened. He immediately sent me to the Headmaster Mr Protheroe (who lived in Weeford Road just one field from our cottage). I waited nervously outside his office until he called me in. To cut a long story short he gave me six of the best with the cane, three whacks on each hand. It was the only time I ever cried when having the cane, not because it hurt, but because I thought it was so unjust when bully boy got off scot-free. My hands and fingers were swollen and throbbing so I put my hands under the cold water tap to get some relief. Dad was right, bully boy never bothered me again.

I suppose most of you played doctors and nurses when you were kids. I was the unlucky one, I was always the ambulance driver and when it came to the exciting bits they would send me for the bandages and when I did get back the kids were all back playing hopscotch. I went through my teenage years thinking sex was done on one leg and when I did get my first chance later in life, behind the Picture House, I fell over.

One of the watering holes near where we lived was the Bassetts Pole Pub, or the Pole as local people called it, and Mom and Dad used to go. Dad played darts and I would watch through the window until it got dark, they would close the curtains because of the wartime blackout law, but most of the locals knew me and they would bring me inside the pub and put me in a corner and cover me up with coats. The local Policeman would visit the pub to make sure no lights were showing and in those days kids were not allowed in pubs, however the Policeman would leave unaware I was hidden under the coats.

I was allowed in the assembly room where on most Saturday nights they had dancing, usually to the Stan Capper Trio. The drummer in the trio would sometimes let me play on his floor tom tom using wire brushes, which I loved doing. Occasionally they would have what they called in those days a 'turn' and on one particular night they had a lady singer who was wearing a long dress. Now, my mother was having a bit of trouble with a fellow who kept trying to chat her up and she kept complaining to my dad about this chap. So, in the end my dad went up to this chap and hit him, down on the floor this chap went. In those days they would sprinkle French chalk on the dance floor to make it slippery and better to dance on. My dad hit this chap and down on the floor he went, sliding on the French chalk and landing with his head between the lady singer's legs, looking up her dress. The lady singer was a true professional and kept on singing.

The Vicar of Canwell came to see my mother to ask her if I would like to join the church choir. I was all for it, at last I was getting into show business. So now I was a Choir Boy, I must have looked a little angel dressed in my white cassock with a hymn book in my hand. The trouble was, I had never had my voice orchestrated (but we did have our cat orchestrated!). Every Sunday I was there in church singing my head off, but I was no singer. When they found out where the noise was coming from they got rid of me.

One Sunday when they passed the collection plate around the congregation a coin fell off the plate, a little boy put his foot on it. The vicar said, 'Foot off little boy.' The little boy said, 'You foot off, I saw it first.'

It was about this time when I started to get really interested in music. Once a week Victor Silvester was on the radio with his orchestra; slow, slow, quick, quick, slow. Dad would let me stay up a bit later to listen to him. We had a piano which I used to play by ear, it did tend to make my ear a bit sore though! I would get the piano stool with a cushion and on the wall we had a brass plaque, I would then take the plaque off the wall and turn it upside down on the cushion. I had made some homemade wire brushes, then I would play along to the radio, which because we didn't have electricity was run off a battery. I found it easy to pick up the rhythms and tempos, I needed a drum teacher but I doubt my parents could have afforded to pay for one. One day my dad came home with a battered old drum kit he had got off a mate of his. Battered it might have been, but to me it was like solid gold. I was so excited, I couldn't wait to put it together and play it, which

I did for hours on end. It must have driven my mom and dad daft, but I must say they never complained.

We didn't have much money in those days and one Christmas Day my mom said, 'We have got your Aunty staying with us. Now, when I ask you if you want some Christmas dinner, you say no Mom I'm not hungry, then I will have enough dinner to give to your Aunt.' So, when Mom asked me did I want some Christmas dinner, as instructed I said, 'No Mom, I'm not hungry.' When it was Christmas pudding time I was all ready for my pudding, so I said, 'I'll have some Christmas pudding, Mom.' She said, 'no you won't you never ate your dinner.'! In our kitchen in one corner, hanging from the ceiling, we had a bunch of mistletoe and in the other corner we had a packet of sage and onion stuffing. Now those who wanted kissing stood under the mistletoe.

One day I was at the bottom of our garden, when I saw in the field next to our garden hanging on a tree was a parachute. I ran and told my mom, she went over the field to the local Post Office and rang the Police. The Police came with some army chaps, they told us it was a German parachute. To my knowledge the German was never found. My mom would have loved to have had that parachute because it was made of a silky material which could have been made into ladies clothes and clothing was rationed during the war years. There was a shop called The Army Navy Stores where we got some of our clothes and I can tell you it was no joke going to school dressed as a Japanese Admiral!

Another incident that happened was when a coach load of German Prisoners of War pulled up outside our kitchen window. They were sent to pick potatoes in the field opposite our kitchen which was only fifteen yards away. The coach drove off and left these Germans, nobody seemed to be in charge of them. What you have to understand is, during the war the very mention of Germans put the fear of God into you, let alone to have them on your doorstep. Now my mother, being of a nervous nature, began to panic so she locked the door and took me upstairs to watch them through the bedroom window. The potatoes had already been lifted out of the ground, so all the Germans had to do was pick the potatoes off the ground and make a Potato Camp (a Potato Camp was a ridge of potatoes all stacked up like a ridge tent, then covered with straw and then covered with soil). This was done to protect them from frost and the bad weather, they would then keep until such time as they were needed.

When lunchtime came the Germans gathered themselves on a piece of grass in front of our kitchen window. They needed a fire to cook their potatoes and close by was our neighbour's hen house, so they kicked in a few side panels for wood for their fire. They also helped themselves to some eggs and a couple of hens also went missing. Now all they needed was something to cook it all in. Before you could say 'Herr Cuts the Barber' they came around to our house to use our outside water tap, I think they thought there was no one at home. They discovered Mom's pots and pans, which they filled with water, and took them to their fire. By now my mother was really uptight, going from one bedroom to another watching these Germans.

Having filled themselves with potatoes, eggs and chicken, they then set about cleaning Mom's pots and pans with soil and water, then returned them to our wash house where they discovered my dad's shaving gear. So they proceeded to stand in line to shave themselves, the razor must have been a bit blunt by the time they had finished. Of course, all this was watched by Mom and I through the bedroom window. So then this well-fed, clean-shaven lot went back to work and later that afternoon the coach returned and took them back to wherever they were billeted.

When Dad came home, Mom told him what had happened and Dad went down the lane to our neighbour and told him about his hen house. Our neighbour was not happy, so much so he fetched his shotgun and was ready to go and shoot these prisoners. He and my dad went down the lane to complain to the farmer, who was only 400 yards away. Fortunately, no one got shot and the next morning the farmer brought a German Officer round to see us and to apologise for his men's behaviour. In fact, the officer spoke excellent English and in spite of everything those German Prisoners meant us no harm, they were just trying to survive. But you try telling that to my mom.

The farmer had a German Prisoner working on the farm, his name was Hans and he used to plough the same field the potatoes where in. He would plough with a big horse called Captain and I used to walk at the side of the horse while Hans was ploughing, I was only a little lad at the time. Hans was glad to be out of the war, he was well-treated and nobody bothered him, he just did his job and was quite happy.

We had a pigsty and Mom and Dad had a pig called Shuster, who I might add was a bit aggressive. The time came when Dad decided to have the pig slaughtered for food so Marsh and Baxter, the butchers, came with a horse and cart to take the pig away. It was loaded into the back of the cart, then the horse pulled the cart up the garden and away they went. Food during the war was rationed and we were only allowed half the carcass, the other half had to go to help feed the nation. When we did get the half carcass back, Dad hung it up from a beam and in the morning he would slice a few rashers off, put them in the frying pan with eggs and sausage, all cooked on the fire of our black lead cast-iron range. That's what I call proper food.

One day when I was about 11 years of age, I read in a musical paper called the *Melody Maker* that the South Staffordshire Regiment at Whittington Barracks were advertising for musicians for their Regimental Band. I got on my bike and cycled all the way to Whittington Barracks to join the Army and be a drummer. When I got to the main gate the guard on duty, complete with his rifle, asked me what I wanted. I said, 'I've come to join the army to be a drummer.' He looked at me then disappeared into the Guard Room. He came back with an Officer who said, 'Hello son, what can we do for you?' I said, 'I've come to join the Army to be a drummer.' 'Well,' said the Officer, 'you're a bit young at the moment but if you come back in a few years time, we would be glad to have you.' When I think back I bet they had a good laugh. Anyway, I got back on my bike and headed for home with my tail between my legs (and that can be painful when you're riding a bike). The funny thing was, I didn't tell my mom and dad that I was going to join the Army.

One day my mom was standing in a queue in one of our local shops, next to my headmaster Mr Protheroe, the very same headmaster who had given me six of the best with the cane. Mom asked him how was I getting on at school? He replied in a very loud voice, 'Mrs Rubery, your son is one of those boys who will end up with a motor bike, with a floozy on the back.' Well, my poor mom was so embarrassed because the people in the queue could hear everything that Mr Protheroe had said!

The first time I ever saw a TV was at the Happy Hour Café opposite The Bassetts Pole Pub. The owner lived in a double-decker bus at the back of the café and was a pal of my dad. The TV screen was 12 inches square, black and white and was showing a Cup Final match between Liverpool and another team which I can't remember. Having never seen a TV before I found it fascinating. The local lads used to go into the Happy Hour and play on the pinball machine, you had to put a threepenny piece into the machine to operate it. The older lads showed me how to fiddle the machine, what they did was insert the coin into the slide then put a piece of sticky tape over the coin, so when the coin was pushed in it operated the machine and when the slide was pulled back the coin was still in the slide, so they would keep getting a free go. Before it was the Happy Hour Café, it was called the Blue Lagoon nightclub. It is now a McDonald's.

My next school was Victoria Road School in the centre of Sutton Coldfield. We had a special bus that took us from Mere Green to Sutton but the Canwell lads still had to get to Mere Green from Canwell in order to catch the bus to Sutton. The Headmaster at Victoria Road was a Mr Gregory and once again discipline was the name of the game. I didn't stay long at this school before we were transferred to Riland Bedford School, still in Sutton Coldfield (now known as Plantsbrook School). The headmaster of Riland Bedford was a Mr Roberts and our teacher was Mr Nobby Harris.

We used to take our dinner money to school and our dinner money monitor would collect the money and put it on a low table in front of the class. Later in the morning an attractive lady would come into the classroom to count and collect the money. Now this lady would lean over the table to sort the money and this meant she showed a lot of cleavage. Well, for us young teenage boys with our hormones beginning to kick in, it made it a good excuse to go to school every day.

In 1950 I was 13 years of age when Grandad Rubery was taken ill and needed to go into hospital. Grandad said, 'I'm not going into any hospital.' My dad said, 'Pop they will make you better.' 'Don't care I'm not going into any hospital.' The night before he was due to go into hospital I shaved his face for him. When I got up next morning Mom and Dad were very upset, Grandad had sadly passed away during the night. He was right when he said that he would not go to hospital. When it came to the funeral Mom and Dad hadn't got enough money, so they had to pay Hazels the Funeral Directors a bit of money each week until the bill was paid in full.

One of my dad's sisters Nelly worked for the McCorquodales in Wolverhampton and when they moved to Helmsdale, in the north of Scotland, Nelly went with them. She eventually met and married a Scotsman and they lived and worked on the game rich 30,000 acre Torrish estate near Helmsdale. Nelly had two sons Jimmy and Angus, Angus went on to become the Gillie of the estate. My cousin Angus taught Prince Charles to fish for salmon in the river Helmsdale, as well as the Queen Mother, in fact the Queen Mother was a very good salmon fisher. Aunty Nelly said Prince Charles was always well dressed, but he did have a hole in his dressing gown. My other cousin Gordon Hickinbotham and his wife Josie gave me a whole page from a newspaper showing cousin Angus with Prince Charles and the Queen Mother salmon fishing in the river Helmsdale. Another frequent visitor was the novelist Barbara Cartland, who had been married on two occasions to two of the McCorquodales.

Chapter 3

FACTORY LIFE

At last it was time for what I had been waiting for, I was now 15 years of age and could leave school, I couldn't wait. I left school with two A levels, one in Woodwork and one in Mathematics so I spent the next five years making wooden rulers! Only joking, I left school with no qualifications, I was not a clever chap at all. What I was good at was practical things like mending things, anything that was mechanical. The Careers Officer secured me a six-year apprenticeship as a millwright at the GEC in Witton, Birmingham (the name millwright is the old-fashioned description for a machine tool fitter). We started work at 7.30 in the morning until 5.18 at night, with a one-hour lunch break, it was a 48 hour week and my wages were £1-17 shillings a week (in today's money it would equate to £1.86p).

I would walk from Canwell to Roughley to catch a bus very early in the morning, on the bus there were other men going to their places of work smoking their Woodbine cigarettes and coughing their lungs up. I would get off the bus at Salford Bridge, which is now Spaghetti Junction, and then walk to Electric Avenue in Witton ready to clock in for 7.30am. All this was a lot to deal with for a 15 year old just out of school. My dad worked in Aston in Birmingham and at night-time he would pick me up at Salford Bridge, so we travelled home together. After a while I think Dad took pity on me and decided to go to work a bit earlier, thus giving me lift and allowing me to stay in bed a bit longer. This was a god send to me and it saved me a lot of time, thanks to my old dad, bless him.

On my first day at work I met another young chap, his name was Michael Poutney, he had started work the week before me and he lived with his parents on the Chester Road, Erdington in Birmingham. We got on well together from the first time we met, we had our lunch breaks together and we became the best of friends which has lasted all of our adult lives. The guys in the workshop called us the two Micks who were always up to mischief.

I had heard that the Royal Warwickshire Regiment Army Cadets in Sutton Coldfield had a band, so I went to see them and told them I was learning to play the drums. That was it, they pushed a military drum into my arms complete with white gloves and a pair of sticks and said 'you're in'. As the weeks went by I was kitted out with a uniform and they taught me to play military style drumming, it takes a bit of practise but I am a bit bow-legged which was a big help. I was at the end of our lane, practising drumming and marching in the field at the side of the lane. One of our neighbours Sammy Blackwell, had a lot of hen houses and lots of chickens and the sound of my drumming must have upset them because they started flying in the air and were kicking up one hell of a row. Sammy must have heard the commotion and he came running out of his cottage and chased me down the lane shaking his fist and shouting abuse at me. I quickly tucked my drum under my arm and ran the 400 yards back to our cottage. My dad told me, when he saw Sammy in the pub, they had a good laugh about it. Obviously Sammy's chickens were not very musical, over the years I've met some audiences who were a bit like those chickens.

Me aged 16. I was Lance Corporal Drummer.

I passed my tests and became an efficient military drummer. We played at fetes and Remembrance Days and I was promoted to Lance Corporal when I was about 16 years old. I was in the Cadets for three years, after which I regrettably had to leave. The reason being that because I was an apprentice, it was in the agreement that I attend Technical College in order to obtain a City and Guilds Certificate in Engineering. Now with working 48 hours a week, studying at college with homework, plus attending Army Cadets, it became too much to cope with. By now I was also riding a motorbike (as my old Headmaster said I would) and getting interested in girls.

When I was about 16, my dad paid to have electricity installed by the MEB in our cottage. In the living room, hanging from the ceiling, was a 100 watt bulb with no lamp shade but when it got dark and the light was switched on to us it was like Blackpool Illuminations. No more paraffin lamps, no more candles to go to bed with. Jimmy Bond (who will be mentioned later) remembers me being all excited telling him that we had got electricity.

Michael Poutney would spend a lot of time with our family, he would cycle from Erdington to our cottage and spend the weekends with us. He considered himself as part of our family, more than his own. On a Saturday night my mom, dad, Michael and I would go to a pub in Hopwas near Tamworth, called The Chequers (now called the Tame Otter). They had a piano player and you could dance, it was here that my mom taught Michael and I how to dance.

Talking about girls, there was a young lady who I will call Miss X, as I wish to protect her identity as she did eventually get married to someone else. Miss X was a very pretty, petite girl with dark hair and I hope she won't mind me saying that she was madly in love with me. I think she thought that one day maybe we would get married which was fair enough, I did think a lot of her, she was a lovely girl. We were courting for quite a while but I got to thinking at the end of my apprenticeship, I was due to go into the Army for two years and I was still a young chap and I didn't want to be tied down.

So, one night when we were in the cinema, I told her I was breaking off our relationship. Oh dear, she was so upset, she cried very loudly and people were looking at us wondering what was wrong. I got her outside and we caught a bus to take her home, she cried all the way home. Once again people on the bus were looking at us wondering why she was so upset. When we got off the bus, we had to walk a little way to her house, where she was sick all over the pavement. I didn't expect it to be like this and I felt so guilty about it all. When I got back to work the girls she worked with sent me bits of paper with messages on them, calling me all the names you could think of, some of the messages suggested that I didn't know who my father was. When I look back on the situation, I can see that I did it all wrong. Some years later I saw her mother and she told me that they had a terrible time with her after we broke up. Who knows in the long run I may have done her a favour?

Michael and I used to go to the Onion Fair near the Aston Villa Football Ground and one time Michael had arranged to meet a young lady who he was keen on. We met the young lady and Michael suggested we went on the Caterpillar, so the three of us got on and sat down, away we went with the young lady sitting in between us. When we had gone round a couple of times the canopy came over us, it was ideal for courting couples all dark under the canopy. I was sitting there when I felt a hand stroking my hand, I thought this is great and I started stroking the hand back, I thought she must fancy me more than Michael. At the end of the ride the canopy opened up to reveal Michael and I holding hands and the young lady sitting between us with her arms folded. She must have thought we were a couple of idiots. Michael and I laughed about that for years after.

When we came off the Caterpillar, we went into the boxing tent. They were announcing that if any man could last three rounds with one of their boxers he could win 10 shillings, or something like that amount. I thought I could do that and I could do with a bit of money. I was just about to volunteer when another fellow beat me to it. Well, the resident boxer knocked hell out of this volunteer, finishing him off in the first round. I quickly changed my mind, money isn't everything. I must have been out of my mind to even think I could last three rounds.

Michael and I went to Ireland for a week's holiday. We flew from Birmingham to Dublin with Air Fungus, the aircraft was a twin-engine Dakota, it was quite old, with outside toilets and Pontius was the Pilot. The wings were thatched and on the side was some graffiti saying 'Romans Go Home'. The crew wore wellington boots in case it rained. I said to Michael, 'Let's sit at the back.' He asked, 'Why?' I said, 'Well, you never hear of these planes reversing into hillsides.' I sat there and I said, 'Those people look like ants.' Michael said, 'They are ants, we haven't taken off yet.' We were bound for Dublin, in fact we landed quite close to Dublin airport. Joking apart, it was the first time we had flown and we enjoyed it immensely.

We were staying at a Butlins Holiday Camp, Hi-de-Hi and all that, it was in a place called Mosney just a few miles south of Dublin. We went into Dublin a couple of times and it was while we were in Dublin that we discovered draught Guinness in a place called Mooney's Bar. The Guinness in Ireland is wonderful, nothing like it is in England.

Meanwhile back at Butlins, one night we were in our chalet when there was a loud knocking on our door and a voice boomed out, 'Have you chaps got any girls in there?' We said no, so they opened the door and threw two girls in. At the end of the week it was time for us to pack our cases and head back to Birmingham. We had a great week in Ireland, we had a lot of fun and a lot of Guinness. Once again we flew back on yet another Dakota Aircraft over the Irish Sea and back to Birmingham.

As already mentioned, I had to attend Technical College and I really enjoyed my time at college studying Engineering. It was while I was in one of the lessons that I was tapping on a pencil case with a pencil, unaware I was doing it (I've always been a knife and fork drummer at the dinner table). The teacher jumped up and ordered me out of the class, so I collected my things and left. When the coffee break came, one of the other lads came up to me and said, 'I saw you get thrown out of the class, I think the teacher was a bit harsh on you. Do you play the drums?' 'Yes,' I replied. He said, 'I'm getting a skiffle group together, do you fancy joining me?' I said, 'that sounds great, count me in.' His name was Keith Cowdrill and his dad owned a bicycle shop on the Soho Road in Handsworth, Birmingham. Keith told me that he already had a piano player and a guitar player. He said he was looking for a Tea Chest Bass player, so I suggested my pal Michael Poutney. I also suggested another pal of mine, who I was at school with, James Bond. James Bond, I hear you say, not the 007 James Bond? This was way before the Bond films, our James Bond was always known as Jimmy Bond and I mentioned him earlier. Jimmy played mandolin and harmonica and was also magic on two wheels, he was into Cycle Speedway and used to ride for the Kingstanding Monarchs. Later in life he became a Motor Cycle Speedway Rider and he even rode for England.

Back to the skiffle group. When we started rehearsing we were playing mostly Lonnie Donegan tunes, Donegan was the king of skiffle. We called ourselves The Sunnysiders and we carried our gear on our motor bikes. Michael tied his Tea Chest Bass with a length of rope to the back of his motor bike, with a broom stale sticking up. Then there was me with drums on my back, drums on my petrol tank, and cymbals and stands sticking out of my side panniers. There I was riding along like a mobile One Man Band, I could have been mistaken for a rag and bone man. Keith did get us a few gigs, places like The Crown and Cushion in Perry Barr, Birmingham.

One night we were booked to play in the interval at The Abbey in Erdington, Birmingham. When the time came for us to perform, we put on our stage clothes that consisted of red shirts and powder blue jeans which were that tight you could tell what religion I was. Having performed and completed our gig, we changed back into our normal clothes and went and mixed with the audience. Later, when the big band was playing, I asked this young lady for a dance. I was chatting to her and nonchalantly asked her, because I was eager to know, 'What did you think of the Skiffle Group?' She replied, 'Weren't they awful?' I said, 'Oh yes, I agree.' What could I say? I was just hoping she didn't recognise me as the drummer. Needless to say I never asked her for another dance.

Me and Michael Poutney.

Chapter 4

ARMY LIFE

I finally completed my six-years apprenticeship with an Intermediate City and Guilds Certificate under my belt, I was now a fully-fledged millwright (machine tool fitter). The 28th of March 1958 was my 21st birthday and what do you think came floating through the letter box? Yes, birthday cards as you would expect, but something else was amongst the cards. It was a buff-coloured envelope with O.H.M.S. printed in bold black letters on the top, which meant ON HER MAJESTY'S SERVICE. It was my call up papers inviting me, or should I say ordering me, to join Her Majesty's Forces. What a birthday present that was.

I was sent a railway pass and told to present myself at the Royal Engineers Camp in Malvern on 10th of April 1958. It did put a dampener on my 21st birthday but I was expecting it. The skiffle group were appearing at the Foseco Club, which was based on the edge of Drayton Manor Park, the night went well even though I fell off my drums, too many drinks. My mom and dad and some friends were in the audience cheering us on. It was the last time that the skiffle group played together. Michael had already gone into the RAF, I was about to go into the Army and Jimmy Bond was also due to go into the Royal Signals Motor Bike Display Team, because of his expertise with motorbikes. So that was the end of the skiffle group.

Before going into the Army, I had to go for a medical at Baggot Street in Birmingham to make sure I was a hundred percent fit for the rigours of service life. We all stood in line, stark naked. The Medical Officer walked up and down the line looking at us, he stopped in front of this weedy looking lad, he looked down at his private parts and said, 'You're not very big down there are you son?' The weedy lad looked up and said, 'We are only going to fight them aren't we, Sir?' The officer asked, 'Could you kill a man?' The weedy lad said, in an effeminate voice, 'Yes Sir, but it would take a couple of weeks.'

The 10th of April arrived and it was time for me to say goodbye to my parents. Dad had already gone to work, so I didn't see him. Mom was so upset at my leaving that she wouldn't come downstairs to say goodbye, so I never saw either of them before I left. I was feeling a bit anxious myself, I was entering into a bit of an unknown adventure like hundreds of other young chaps.

So, off I went on this new adventure. I eventually arrived at Malvern Railway Station, there was a lot of other chaps also there and an Army truck turned up to take us to the foot of the Malvern Hills, where the Royal Engineers Training Camp was situated. So began my two years National Service in The Corps of the Royal Engineers. A Royal Engineer is known as a Sapper, they say once a Sapper always a Sapper and that's very true. The REs have a long heritage that not many other corps could rival, they say the REs date back to William the Conqueror.

Over the next two weeks we were kitted out with bedding and uniforms, then the trip to the dreaded Barbers shop, where they cut your hair right down to the canvas. We had the odd teddy boy, with the Tony Curtis hair do, their pride and joy and they were panicking about their lost locks. Any hair you could get under your hat was yours, any hair outside was non-existent. Our uniforms were tailored to fit and we were taught how to press them and also how to bull our boots. I was lucky having spent three years in the Royal Warwickshire Cadets, I could already do all of these things. Then there was the Parade Ground Drill, better known as Square Bashing. Once again, I could do this, so I fitted in quite easily.

After two weeks we were taken to Number 9 training camp at Southwood Cove in Farnborough, Hampshire. Before I go any further, let me tell you about an Army pay packet, it contained 27 shillings a week (£1.35p in today's money). Back to the story, and things began to get a lot tougher at this camp. If it moved you saluted it and if it was stationary you polished it. We lived in wooden huts called Spiders, they had a long corridor with rooms going off the corridor like a spider's legs, hence the name Spider. Our Spider was at the end, so we were furthest from the road, where we assembled to march down the road to the cookhouse for our meals. We had a Royal Artillery shell which was hanging from the roof and when it was time for us to assemble for our meals, the NCOs would clang this shell and we would go to the road and line up.

With us being at the end we were always in the furthest queue and last to be served. A few yards down the road the NCOs would give the order to turn left, then march a short 50 yards and we came to the cookhouse, sometimes the NCOs would march us past the left turn, then about turn us which meant us chaps at the back got served first for a change.

One day when the brass shell was sounded, I managed to get out onto the road first, so I was all set to get to the cookhouse and be one of the first to be served lunch. As we were marching down the road, it soon became apparent that it was going to be one of those times when the NCOs were going to march us past the left turn, which meant those lads at the back where going to be at the front of the queue. So, I took matters into my own hands and shouted in a loud voice 'Left Wheel!' and fifty soldiers turned left. I must say I didn't fool them, we were halted and an NCO's voice boomed out, 'Who's the bright spark who shouted Left Wheel?' Well I had to own up, all the lads including the NCOs were laughing their socks off at the cheek of it. I was put to the back and in addition told to report to the cookhouse Sergeant who promptly put me to work. He gave me a hundred weight of onions to peel and chop up. Three hours later my eyes looked like I had just completed 10 rounds with a heavy weight boxer.

Another situation I got myself in to was when I was walking along the camp main road and a very loud hoarse sounding voice boomed in my ear, falsely accusing me of having my hands in my pockets. It was a snotty-nosed Lance Corporal who looked about 12 years of age. The stripes on his arm looked new and the power had obviously gone to his head. All the way down the road he kept on about me having my hands in my pockets but I kept on walking and ignoring him, which seemed to make him worse. When I got to my Spider I went in the back way and when we were out of sight of anyone, I turned on him. I'm afraid I lost my temper and I grabbed him by the throat and threw him across a pile of coal, I told him in no uncertain terms what I thought of him and to go away in the best colourful language I could think of. I think he understood because he was off like a shot with the back of his uniform covered in coal dust. When I got back inside our Spider I sat on my bed and put my head in my hands, what had I done? I could be in real trouble. He was going to come back with the RPs and I would end up in the Nick, to assault an NCO was a serious offence. So, I waited and waited and guess what? Nothing happened, I got away with it and I never saw him again.

I used to make a bit of money on the side because I was able to bull boots and press uniforms. Some of the lads who couldn't get the hang of doing these things would say 'Brummie, press my uniform' or 'Brummie, bull my boots and I'll give you two shillings.' (10p in today's money).

We had an NCO who slept in our hut and snored liked the mating call of a Canadian elk. The lads who slept by him got that fed up with his snoring that one night they picked up his bed, with him still in it, and carried him outside to the middle of the parade ground and left him there still fast asleep. As any serviceman will tell you the Parade Ground is sacred, if the RSM had seen him, there would be hell to pay. When he woke up I bet he was panicking, after that he was too scared to go to sleep, but he took it all in good spirit.

Having completed our basic square bashing and rifle drill, we went on the rifle range firing 303 Lee Enfield rifles and Bren Guns, which were machine guns. It was while we were on the ranges that I was detailed to be on guard, two hours on and four hours off. It was the early hours of the morning and it was my turn to do two hours guard duty, after a short time I spotted a fire in the woods quite close to our camp and I might add, also our Armoury. Within a few seconds another fire started, I quickly called the Guard Commander, who then called out the duty officer. On seeing these very suspicious fires he immediately ordered all us lads that were on guard duty to fix bayonets and surround the Armoury. They thought that someone was trying to get us out of the camp to put out the fires, so they could get into the camp and rob our Armoury which was full of all sorts of firearms and ammunition. So, there we were with our bayonets on the end of our rifles, if anybody had said 'boo' to me they would have had six inches of bayonet stuck in them. We were there till daylight, which we were glad to see. We never did find out the truth about the cause of those fires.

We did a Watermanship course at Hawley Lakes with the objective to learn all about building bridges across rivers. We were taught how to row boats, we also had assault boats made of canvas and wood with a plywood bottom which folded up to a few inches, making them easy to carry. When they were pulled up to their full height and put on water, we then fitted a Seagull outboard motor on the back and could then travel up and down rivers. The REs were responsible for building Bailey Bridges across rivers, which we practised until we could do it with our eyes closed.

Having completed our Watermanship course our next course was Demolition, Booby Traps and Land Mines at Longmoor. We were taught how to blow up railway tracks, the correct way to plant anti-tank mines and how to find anti-personnel mines with a bayonet, even how to find booby traps. Another important job the REs did was bomb disposal, steel girders can be cut in half with explosives, if you know how to do it.

Finally, after 12 weeks of intensive training, it was time to receive the sought-after blue lanyard, which was given to the Royal Engineers for bravery a long time ago. This was worn on the right shoulder with pride and also showed we were fully-fledged Royal Engineers. After the passing-out parade I was approached by two NCOs who asked me if I would like to go on a Cadre Course, to train to be an NCO. This meant I would have been promoted and earned more money. I suppose it was an honour to be considered for the job, they must have seen something in me for them to think I was NCO material and I was always smartly turned out. However, I turned them down because I had already volunteered to go abroad, I had itchy feet and I badly wanted to see something of the world. My kit bag was packed, I was given a week's leave. We were issued with train passes and given a lift in an army truck to the railway station.

I think I should mention at this point that I was a National Serviceman, just in case there are younger people reading this who do not know what National Service was. When a young man reached the age of 18 he had to go into one of the Armed Forces by law, to do his bit for Queen and Country. If you were an apprentice, like me, you were deferred until you were 21 years old, after you had finished your apprenticeship then you went into the Armed Forces, and that was the law of the land at that time.

Chapter 5

SEEING A BIT OF THE WORLD

So, there I was on a well-earned seven days leave, when yet another buff coloured letter came through the letter box marked O.H.M.S. informing me that I had another seven days leave and then I had to report to Harwich Docks. I was due to set sail across the North Sea to the Hook of Holland, enroute to Osnabruck in Germany. The sea voyage was extremely rough and stormy and as we travelled through the night the lads were being seasick all over the place. I was one of the lucky ones because I have never been seasick. One minute we were on top of the waves looking down, the next minute we were on the bottom looking up at the waves. We had bunk beds three or four bunks high and if you stuck your head out of your bunk you were in danger of being vomited on. The ship's crew were kept busy hosing down the decks to wash the vomit away and the trip took about seven or eight hours to travel 122 miles.

On our arrival in Holland, we boarded a train bound for Germany. It was the Blue Train, a British military train, which ran from the Hook through Rotterdam on to Osnabruck. Robert Barracks was our destination, originally it was a German Barracks called Winkelhausen, and we were based there for the summer of 1958. We were posted to 36 Regiment, 57 Field Squadron, 3 Troop, Corps of Royal Engineers.

During the Second World War, Osnabruck was all but destroyed as it was bombed on a regular basis. It was on the RAF flight path from London to Berlin and on the way back from Berlin the RAF would drop any leftover bombs on Osnabruck thus causing a lot of damage. During our stay in Osnabruck, I passed my A2 Fitters Trade Test and my Test piece was put on show in a cabinet. I was quite proud of that. So now I was a Field Engineer B3 and a Fitter A2, which was a higher trade than our Troop Sergeant.

One time we were taken to the River Weser where we had to build a Bailey Bridge across the river. I can remember that we built the bridge and made a good job of it, as we were admiring our hard work, up came one of our officers who said, 'Well done chaps you've done a great job, now let's get it dismantled' and then he walked away. Building these bridges was backbreaking. They were portable prefabricated truss bridges, one panel was 10 foot long and 5 foot high and it took six men to carry one panel. So, when I say it was hard work it really was. I can't remember how long it was, but it could have been something like 100 yards long. We were working through the night and when we had finished we had had enough I can tell you.

There are a few stories I can remember while I was in Osnabruck. On one occasion we were ordered to stand by our beds for an identity parade. A young German girl was brought round to see if she could identify the chap who had done something or other to her. I don't know what had happened to her, but it wasn't me. I did have a German girlfriend, well she was half German she only shaved under one arm, she was a redhead no hair just a red head. Her name was Girder, it was an old German name Girder. Being a redhead I called her Rusty, that's right Rusty Girder! We went to a Bier Keller and afterwards she took me back to her flat and I made love to her, afterwards I said to her in nine months' time you will have a little boy and you can call him Adolf if you like. She said in three weeks' time you will have a rash and you can call it German Measles if you like (joke).

I had toothache one time and our medical officer sent me down town to a German dentist. Well, this German dentist removed my tooth and in doing so he nearly pulled my head off in the process. I was in uniform so he knew where I was from, perhaps he was trying to get his own back due to our RAF dropping their bombs.

The food in the cookhouse was very good and it was here I was introduced to Frankfurter sausages. There was a big stainless steel pan full of them, you could just help yourself, they were great with a bread roll and a bit of mustard.

After our duties we would sometimes catch a tram to go down town to have a drink in one of the pubs. By now we had learned a bit of the German language, enough to get by, and we would go in our civvy clothes so not to be too conspicuous to anyone that may had a drink and want to cause trouble, not that I remember there being any trouble. We got talking to a German chap one night who spoke English and he told us that their Luftwaffe had flattened our cities like London, Coventry and Birmingham. In fact, he was sort of bragging about it. After he had gone, another German chap who had heard what the other chap had said, came up to us and said, 'Don't take too much notice of him, your RAF did just as much damage in Germany.' We all agreed that it was a great pity that there had to be wars, these two chaps were a lot older than us, more our fathers age.

When you ordered a drink, the Barman would put a mark on your beer mat and when you had finished the barman would add up the marks and tell you how much you had to pay, all very trusting. I don't know if they still mark the beer mats, the last time I was in Germany back in the 1990s, I don't seem to remember them doing it then.

At the end of the summer, we were told we were going back to England. So, we packed our kit bags and we boarded the Blue Train yet again, to made our way back to England. This time, thankfully, the North Sea was a lot calmer. We were taken to Invicta Lines in Maidstone, Kent but we were only at Maidstone for a short time while we were kitted out with our Tropical Kit (olive green uniforms) in readiness to be shipped out to Christmas Island in the Pacific Ocean, just off the Equator. There are two Christmas Islands, one in the Indian Ocean which is more for tourists and our Christmas Island close to the Equator where the Nuclear bombs were tested in the 1950s/60s. The Polynesians have renamed the island and it is now called Kiritimati, which means Christmas in Polynesian.

Whilst I was in Maidstone, I met a young lady a pretty blond, I will refer to her as Miss Y, to protect yet another lady's identity. We dated a number of times, but

Me in Osnabruck, Germany, 1958.

with me shortly going off to the Pacific, nothing came of it at that time (more about Miss Y later).

One night, just before we were due to leave Maidstone, four of us lads went down town for a drink and being young fit soldiers we could do our fair share of drinking. Having done our best to drink Maidstone dry, it was time to get back to camp. On our way back, our bladders were at bursting point, so we decided to nip into one of the alleyways between the houses known as Stacy's Passage. So, there we were all four of us lined up relieving ourselves, it was like high tide in springtime, running down the alley into the road. We were in mid flow when suddenly a torch light lit up the scene, it was a Policeman who was walking by and spotted the torrent running into the gutter. He promptly booked all four of us, but he had to wait until we had finished first.

It was not long after the Policeman had booked us that we were loaded up on coaches and taken to Maidstone Railway Station, then taken by train to London and then to RAF Hendon where our kit bags were weighed. We were given an advance out of our wages, we didn't get money for nothing. From Hendon we were taken to Heathrow Airport to catch a plane to New York. Being October in the 1950s it was prone to foggy weather and on this occasion the fog had come down, so we were hanging around the Airport waiting for the fog to lift. Also at the Airport waiting to go to New York was Joan Collins, the film star, and her sister Jackie Collins who were also held up because of the fog. One or two of our lads asked Joan for her autograph and she willingly obliged, she even sat amongst us and chatted to the lads. I thought it was very nice of her. There was no way we were able to take off with this fog, so they took us back to Hendon for the night.

The next morning, we went back to Heathrow and the fog had cleared, so we were all set to board a plane for New York. Joan Collins had also returned to the Airport and she waved goodbye to us as we left. Our plane was a United Airways DC7 Seven Seas, it was not a jet it was a 4-engine propeller plane. The flight took 12 hours and we flew over Ireland and across the Atlantic Ocean. While we were flying over the Atlantic we flew into a storm, the plane was going up and down in the turbulence. The pilot came on the intercom, telling us to fasten our safety belts and we began to get worried, the turbulence was quite bad. However, after a while conditions got better and we were told to unfasten our belts.

We arrived at Idlewild Airport, as it was called in those days, it has since been renamed John F. Kennedy Airport. We were not allowed off the aircraft until an American Medical Officer had checked our Army Medical Records (which we carried with us) to make sure we had had our appropriate injections to enter foreign countries. Eventually we were allowed off the plane, where we boarded a coach and were taken into New York. I was amazed at the size of the motorways or freeways as they called them. We were taken to the Governor Clinton Hotel, named after the first Governor of New York State, which was opposite Pennsylvania Station.

Derek Green and I shared a room together, not that we stayed in it. Derek had a mate who worked in New York, he hadn't seen him in a long time, but he had kept in touch with him. Derek had his phone number so rang him from our hotel, his mate gave him directions on how to get to the Bronx, the area where he lived. Derek asked me if I wanted to go with him and I said, 'Great yes, I'll go.' We were told to get a taxi to the Bronx, but to get there we had to go through Harlem and none of the taxi drivers would take us because back in the 1950s there was a big problem in the USA concerning the black population and the white population and Harlem was seen as the black people's area. Eventually we did get a taxi driver to take us because he lived in the Bronx. As we were driving through Harlem, the taxi driver said, 'Guys, if we break down here we are dead.' So we were praying that we didn't break down, perhaps the driver was just trying to scare us, I don't know.

Derek had arranged to meet his pal at a bar in the Bronx, which the taxi driver knew of. Derek and his pal were pleased to see each other and that's when the drinks began to flow. With Derek and I in our uniforms, it wasn't long before the locals realised we were British and started buying us drinks. Before long the inevitable happened and everybody was worse for wear with drink. We ended up at Derek's mate's flat, which was situated in one of those high rise type buildings. The next thing I remember was waking up in the early hours of the morning on a fire escape overlooking New York, which was all lit up in the distance. I was so cold, I had no uniform jacket on, I went through a door back into the building to see my jacket hanging on someone's flat door handle. My army belt was on another handle and my beret on another door. I quickly gathered my stuff and tried to find out where Derek was. I could hear a lot of laughter, which led me to the right door. Apparently in my drunken haze, I had said I was going home. Well, I was only 3,000 miles away from home so it would have been a good walk back.

Time was getting on and it was time for us to get back to the hotel. We struggled to get a taxi to take us back to the hotel, in the end we had to bribe one and on our way we passed the Yankee Stadium. When we arrived back at the hotel we began to panic, our guys were already getting on an American army bus, ready to travel to the airport. We had to ask the bus driver to wait while we dashed in to get our kit bags. A few more minutes and we would have missed the bus and would have been in serious trouble, and that's putting it lightly.

When we got to the airport we boarded our plane bound for San Francisco in California approximately 2,600 miles away. We had been airborne for a few minutes when the pilot spoke to us on the tannoy, inviting us to look out of the port side windows to see an amazing sight, the spike of the Empire State Building sticking out of some low lying clouds as we flew over New York. All we could see was the spike, it looked really weird, if only we had cameras like there are in today's world, what a picture it would have made. We flew from one side of America to the other side, almost 3,000 miles, across places such as The Salt Flats, Nevada and Salt Lake City, and then onto San Francisco.

We had to change planes at San Francisco to Hawaiian Airlines, all our luggage had to be transferred from one plane to another and we boarded a DC6, still not a jet, another 4-engine propeller plane. The Hawaiian Air Hostesses were beautiful, they wore flowered sarong dresses and the finishing touch was a flower behind their ears. The meaning of the flower is, if a girl wears a flower behind her right ear, she is single, if the flower is worn behind the left ear she is married or already taken. It's like wearing a ring on your left hand.

We left San Francisco and started our 2,400 mile journey across the blue Pacific Ocean to Honolulu. We were flying at about 10,000 feet and as we looked down the sea was so blue and beautiful to see. Many hours later we landed at Honolulu and when we got off the plane, we couldn't help but notice the heat. I thought it was a beautiful place, all the tropical plants and greenery. I sent my mom and dad a postcard with a bare-chested Hawaiian girl on the front, I've still got that card. My mother kept all my letters and cards that I sent all those years ago and when she passed away they came back to me.

The plane was refuelled and we got back on board, next stop Christmas Island another 1,400 miles to fly over that beautiful blue sea.

Chapter 6

CHRISTMAS ISLAND (KIRITIMATI)

With many flying hours under our belts, we finally arrived at Christmas Island just off the Equator. As we flew over we could see the whole of the Island, it was 30 miles long by 15 miles wide at its widest point, and quite narrow at its narrowest point. It looked so small from the plane, stuck in the middle of the Pacific Ocean.

We landed at the airfield and when we got off the plane the heat hit us like a sledgehammer, we were as close to the Equator as you can get and the temperature was in the region of 90 to 95 degrees. We were shown to our tents and were so glad to change out of our Battle Dress uniforms and into our Tropical gear. We were told to keep covered up so that the sun didn't burn us up and over our beds we had mosquito nets, which we used at first, then never bothered with them again. Those mosquitoes are very clever, they came in twos, one would lift up the net and the other one would fly in and get you.

The sun belted down on us then reflected off the coral and got us again. Christmas Island (Kiritimati) is a coral atoll, in fact it is the largest coral atoll in the world (coral atolls are formed by underwater volcanoes) and surrounding the Island was a spectacular coral reef.

In the late afternoon when the heat of the day had eased we had compulsory sunbathing, so long on your back and so long on your front. This was done to gradually acclimatise us to the heat and after a few weeks we began to get used to it, but I did feel sorry for the lads who had red hair, they tended to suffer the most. The guys who had been there for some time were an ebony colour, they called us lads who were not tanned Moonies.

We were billeted at the airfield and could see the Dakotas and Hastings aircraft taking off and landing. The RAF ran the airfield and the cookhouse, I

The four Stacy's Passage Gang. I'm the one on the left.

always thought the food was good. We had been on the Island a few weeks when we had a letter from the Maidstone Magistrates Court addressed to Sappers Rubery, Green, Whally and Langdon ordering the four of us to appear at the Maidstone Court charged with urinating in Stacy's Passage. I don't think Stacy was very pleased about it. Of course, it was to do with the time we were booked for relieving ourselves and the Maidstone Camp must have received the letter and then forwarded it to us. Anyway, we were 11,000 miles away and there was no way we were going to attend and never heard any more about it. Whether the army sorted it out, we will never know. We pinned the letter to the tent pole and it was a source of amusement for the other lads in the tent.

At night we used to get these big brown flies flying around the light bulb and then the lizards would run up the tent pole and catch them with their tongues. When the lights were switched off, sometimes the land crabs would come in the tent, we knew they were there because we could hear the tap, tap, tap of their claws on the roof felting which was on the floor of the tent.

We lived a very rough existence. The toilet was a bucket with a seat on top and in the bucket were chemicals that broke up the solids, with the heat these buckets could smell a bit. If we did a bit of washing we had a 50 gallon drum cut in half filled with water, the coral underneath was soaked in diesel oil and set alight to boil the water, we then threw in a bit of Daz washing powder for good luck. To be fair, the island did have a Laundry, where we had our bedding and clothes laundered.

On Christmas Day morning in 1958 we were woken up by our officers and NCOs with tea and coffee, whisky and rum. It's the tradition in the services that on Christmas Day officers and NCOs wait on the lower ranks. When it was Christmas lunchtime, once again we were waited on by our officers and NCOs. We were given a Christmas Menu, which I still have, with some of the lads' autographs on it. The food was very good, thanks to the RAF.

On Boxing Day, the cookhouse gave us big brown paper bags filled with sandwiches, cans of beer and bits and pieces to eat. We then got onto the back of a 3-ton Bedford truck and then they took us to Ground Zero. Now Ground Zero was the bottom of the column of a Nuclear explosion. This was the site where they suspended a basket from balloons, many feet above the ground, and inside the basket was a Nuclear Bomb, it was then detonated above the ground.

As we approached Ground Zero the vegetation grew less and less until as far as your eyes could see the ground was black, just burnt black. When we got off the truck there were bits of metal and all sorts of things which had been completely destroyed. We were picking things up off the ground and eating our sandwiches, drinking our beer and if you think about it now, it was not a very healthy place to be. A Nuclear bomb had been detonated just a few months before we got there and radiation could still have been hanging about in that area for all we knew.

On New Year's Day 1959, I woke up with a terrible pain in my left ear, I was told to go to the main camp hospital so I hitched a lift on the back of a 4-wheel drive 3-ton tip up truck. The hospital was run by the RAF and the medics looked in my ear and told me I had Singapore Ear so they gave me an injection and put drops in my ear, which did take the pain away. Apparently, Singapore Ear is a fungal infection in the ear canal, which is more common in tropical countries. I still have trouble with my left ear to this day.

It came up on the notice board that if any musicians or entertainers were interested in taking part in a show, they should report to main camp. After work I hitched a lift to main camp and found where the rehearsals were being held. In charge was a guy called Eddie Buchanan, if I remember rightly he also played the drums, but I'm not a hundred percent sure of that. He was also the Disc Jockey on Christmas Island Radio, playing requests for the lads. Anyway, I played a couple or three numbers with the keyboard player while Eddie sang. I didn't get the job as they didn't need a drummer they had one already. So that was the end of that. Or so I thought. Eddie Buchanan, on leaving the services, went singing professionally and when he came to the Midlands I played drums for him a couple of times in the early 1980s. We reminisced about our stay on Christmas Island and he told me he was working on The Benny Hill Show. The next time I worked with him, he was doing a comedy act with his wife. He sadly died when he was only 47 with heart trouble.

Anyway, back to my failed audition on Christmas Island. When I got outside I realised I hadn't got a lift back to the airfield, so I had to walk. By now it was dark, pitch black and there were no proper roads, only coral roads. So I started to walk, Christmas Island was basically a coconut plantation, so I was walking through the coconut trees. As I was walking I could hear scurrying behind me, this went on for a few miles, a bit unnerving to say the least. About a mile from the airfield a Land Rover stopped and an officer gave me a lift the rest of the way.

In the New Year of 1959 we were moved from the airfield to Port London and onto HMS Resolution, which was on dry land, it was named after Captain Cook's ship. Captain Cook discovered Christmas Island on Christmas Eve 1777 and went ashore on Christmas Day, hence the name Christmas Island.

So now we were based with the Navy, although we were all mixed together: Army, Navy, RAF, Fijian Army and Fijian Navy. Our tents were close to one of the lagoons and on the other side of the lagoon was the Gilbertese Village. We were not allowed in their village, it was out of bounds, but the road from the Port to Main Camp ran through the middle of the village so we passed through regularly. Sometimes on a Sunday morning, our only day off, I would go for a walk on my own through the village. The little Gilbertese kids, even the women, would wave to you.

On one such Sunday I took a walk through the village to another lagoon that I knew, on the side of this lagoon there were two Gilbertese chaps who had caught a squid and were cooking it in what looked like coconut leaves, over a small fire. They offered me some, but I turned it down. The Gilbertese people were lovely, they lived in what I would call grass huts, their toilets were 50 yards or more away in another lagoon, which we named Shit Creek. To get to their toilets they walked along planks of wood which were supported by wooden

Me on one of my
Sunday morning walks.

34

stumps, keeping the planks above the water. The toilet itself was also a grass hut on stilts above the lagoon, inside were planks of wood that they sat on, and their poo poos dropped into the lagoon. The tide would come and wash it away, hence the name Shit Creek. That was one lagoon we did not swim in.

Whilst on the subject of swimming, I couldn't swim at that time. Our tents were quite close to a lagoon so we could roll out of bed and a few yards away was a nice clear lagoon. The water was always warm, like a warm bath. Like I said I couldn't swim so the lads in our tent taught me in no time at all, it made it a lot easier to learn in warm water. The water was very clear and the fish would come right up to your face. However, you did have to lookout for the big guys like sharks and manta rays, they say manta rays (not to be confused with the deadly sting rays) are normally friendly to swim with and are very intelligent and can live for many years. I found a manta ray washed up on the beach quite close to our tent, when we measured it was 10 foot 4 inches from tip to tip, but they normally grow much larger, I took a photograph of it.

The cookhouse was run by the Navy and the food had gone down in quality due to the state of the cookhouse. Our number one troop REs got to work to extend and rebuild the cookhouse and the food improved immensely. At night, on our way back from the NAAFI tent, the cooks would leave some snacks of food

Mantra Ray, measuring 10 foot 4 inches across.

on a table outside. We could help ourselves to a nice bit of supper and it was here that I first tasted watermelon.

We had an outdoor cinema, which consisted of planks of wood to make a screen which was painted white, and a small shed to house the projector. We sat on wooden benches with our cans of beer to watch the films, but because it was outside, we had to wait until it got dark. One of the films I remember seeing was *Annie Get Your Gun* staring Betty Hutton and Howard Keel, which was first shown in 1950. It was outside but it was not cold, we had warm tropical nights. It was here, one day, that we were assembled and made to take an oath about anything that we saw on the Island we kept to ourselves. It was to do with The Official Secrets Act. But I never did see anything anyway.

When the Gilbertese went fishing it was a sight to see, the whole village turned out. The men would take a net into the lagoon and form a big semi-circle up to their chests in the water. The women and kids would then start beating the water with sticks from the shore towards the net, to drive the fish into the net. The men would then start closing the net into a circle and pull it into the shore where it would be teeming with fish. I remember seeing the sun shining on the silvery scales of those fish in the net, loads of them, enough fish to feed the whole village.

The outdoor cinema club.

Chapter 7

WORK, WORK AND MORE WORK

Our troop was 3 Troop and we had rather different jobs. We built very large storage sheds which required a lot of heavy foundations plus a lot of steel erecting. These sheds were 135 feet long and 50 feet wide, the other sheds were 75 feet long and 50 feet wide. There was a lot of concreting to contend with, so we were shovelling concrete in 90 something degrees of heat. Having laid the concrete, we covered it with rolls of hessian cloth, then sprayed water over it to stop

The cement mixer gang. That's me on the left.

the sun drying it too quickly and causing it to crack. Having laid the foundations we started steel erecting, we would sometimes work from 7.30am till 6pm at night. These sheds were used to store the Garrison's food and the NAAFI supplies.

We built a Mineral Water Factory which provided tonic water, ginger ale, and lemonade for the Island. Then I was placed on a job building sea defences for the Island as the sea was washing the shore away, this involved pile driving steel pipes into the sea shore and into the sea. We then had to cut down coconut trees, which we placed between the steel pipes, a bit like you see at seaside resorts, only these of ours were more robust to deal with the rigours of the Pacific Ocean waves. Helping us to cut down these trees were some guys from the Fijian Army, they were great guys and they knew how to chop down trees. Coconut trees are solid and they were tough to cut. There was no shortage of coconuts when we needed a drink, we chopped the top off the nut and drank the milk, it tasted lovely in the heat of the day.

I was then given a job on my own, I had to build a Pumping Station on the edge of a lagoon. The idea was to make a reservoir, so when the tide came in it filled the reservoir, which meant there was water all the time for the pump to pump the water when needed to wherever it had to go. To make the reservoir I filled hessian bags full of concrete and built high walls, just high enough for the

Me holding a coconut, standing on a tree I had just chopped down.

What a poser.

tide when it came in to go over the top and fill my reservoir. This took me several days to complete, the second day before I had any height to my wall, I turned up in the morning to find a 4 foot shark that had come in with the tide and when the tide had gone back out it had got stuck behind my wall and had died through lack of water. So, I dragged it out and I kicked some of its teeth out, which I still have somewhere. Sharks teeth are triangular in shape, very handy for ripping its prey apart. It was a sand shark and they grow to about 10 foot long and only live for about seven years. This one must have been young, only being 4 foot in length.

Another task we were given was to pick coconuts for the Gilbertese. The Copra Boat would visit the Island to collect coconuts (I've already mentioned that Christmas Island was a coconut plantation) so to help the Gilbertese we were detailed to harvest the nuts. Our officers told us that the troop that picked the most could have free beer for the night. The outer husk of a coconut is called Copra and is stripped off the nut to make things like coconut matting. All day long we were loading 3-ton trucks with coconuts and in turn the trucks took them to the quayside then loaded them onto landing crafts to be taken over the reef to the Copra Boat. Truckload after truckload we picked and by the end of the day 3 Troop had picked the most, so we had free beer for the night.

Me picking coconuts.

The weather on the Island was quite stable, but we did have a storm one time when the coconut trees were bending over with the wind and rain. It rained so hard that our tents got flooded and we couldn't go to our work sites, in fact it was so bad the Navy came round with a barrel and gave us all a good noggin of rum.

When the weather was normal, some days we were sprayed with DDT from a light aircraft that flew just above the trees, it was done to kill the flies and creepy crawlies. The trouble was it fell on us as well, you could feel it dropping on your bare body as the only clothes we wore were a bush hat, a pair of boots and a pair of shorts. We also had DDT powder that we sprinkled in our beds to kill the slugs that sometimes got in there. Now DDT has since been banned because it's a health hazard.

We did get a bit of recreational enjoyment as we played a lot of sports including football, basketball, hockey and boxing. With the boxing they asked for volunteers to join the Boxing Team and it will be no surprise that I volunteered. We started training, getting up early in the morning when it was still dark, and running through the Gilbertese Village and onwards for several miles, then turning around and running all the way back again. Then into the showers and off to the cookhouse in time for breakfast. This went on for several weeks until we were very fit.

Finally, the big night came and the boxing show was being held at Main Camp and staged outdoors. The boxing ring was flood lit and looked quite impressive in the tropical night, whoever was responsible for organising it had really gone to town, but that's what you would expect from the military. It was a big occasion for everyone on the Island. At the ringside sat the Officers dressed in their best tropical uniforms, then the Warrant Officers, and Senior NCOs and so on down to the lower ranks.

Bout after bout was fought, then came my turn. I was fighting at Welterweight and I wore a pair of shorts and a pair of plimsolls, no head gear and no gum shield. I was escorted from the dressing room to the ring, I sat in my corner while the MC introduced me. Then he introduced my opponent who was a guy called Ferguson who was also an RE. We had three rounds to fight lasting three minutes each round. My corner man was another RE, Sam Weller, who told me to take it easy in the first round and weigh him up. The first round he came at me like a ton of bricks, nobody had told him to take it easy in the first round. I know why they called him Ferguson, he came at me like a tractor (Ferguson Tractors) he hammered me in the first round. I sat in my corner and my second said, 'You're doing okay, he's not laid a glove on you yet.' I said, 'Keep an eye on the Referee then because somebody is knocking the hell out of me.' I spent that much time on the ropes, they called me washing-line. The second round he knocked me down twice, I was bleeding from the nose and

The morning after the boxing, I look a bit bruised.

mouth. Once again I sat in my corner, I looked into the crowd and I saw this face that I seemed to recognise, I should have, it was mine. He knocked me that far out of the ring I had to pay to get back in. In fact, I spent that much time on my back I was advertising the local fish and chip shop on the soles of my feet. They called me Rembrandt because I spent that much time on the canvas. By the third and final round I was getting a bit fed up with being knocked from pillar to post, so I came out of my corner like a wounded animal and got stuck into him. I cut him under his left eye, then I cut him under his right eye, then the Referee took the knife off me. In fact, I did win the last round, but joking apart, he was a better boxer than me. In those days in the army you could be boxing a professional and not know it.

I also played basketball and football for the troop. We played against the RAF, Fijian Navy, Fijian Army and even the Gilbertese had a team. The Gilbertese didn't quite understand the rules of the game, they knew they had to get the ball between the goal posts, but to get the ball they would knock you clean off your feet then pick you up, dust you down and smile at you. They played in their bare feet and that was off putting, they were not very tall but very broad, the Referee's whistle would seized up with overwork.

By now we had better living accommodation in the form of wooden huts. An old mate of mine Ron Barley from Hull (we were in Germany and Christmas Island together) who I am still in contact with, told me that these wooden huts came in flat packs all the way from Hull. When we moved into the huts it was like the Ritz after living in tents for so long.

We did have a very sad occasion when one of our lads passed away. His name was McDermott and if I remember rightly, he died in the early evening and we were told that the funeral would be the next day and it was going to be a burial at sea. We understood the reason for the hasty burial was due to the heat, so we had to quickly bull our boots and press our uniforms. The next day we assembled at the quayside where a landing craft was waiting. A 3-ton truck came with McDermott's body on the back, they carried it onto the craft and placed him on the chute then covered him with a Union Jack Flag. On the craft was a Padre who performed a religious service and then the landing craft went over the reef and buried him out at sea. Later that afternoon it came up on our daily orders that Sapper McDermott had been buried at sea, so many degrees longitude and so many degrees latitude. He was married and his wife had travelled as far as Honolulu when they turned her around and sent her back home.

In April 1959 Prince Philip came to visit the Island, so royal preparations had to be made. I was picked to be on the Royal Engineers Guard of Honour for Prince Philip and so was my mate Ron Barley. It's an honour to be chosen to be on a Royal Guard of Honour but it does have its drawbacks, you rehearse your drill movements time and time again until you are perfect. We were issued with brand-new olive green uniforms which consisted of tropical jacket and tropical shorts, navy blue hose tops complete with the Royal Engineers flash, puttees and of course boots which were bulled up until they looked like mirrors. Our new uniforms were tailored to fit then laundered exactly three times.

In charge of all this was Regimental Sergeant Major Kite, he was a very strict Second World War ex-soldier. We called him Kipper Kite not to his face, needless to say. The day came when the Royal Yacht Britannia anchored off the seaward side of the reef and Prince Philip himself came to the quayside in one of the Royal Yacht's Barges with the Royal Yachtsmen looking very smart. Prince Philip came ashore dressed in his white naval uniform and was escorted around the Naval Guard of Honour, the RAF Guard of Honour and the Royal Engineers Guard of Honour. He walked past and looked at us with a smile, in fact he was quite relaxed. He was shown around the work sites and told what we had achieved on the Island. They also flew him in a helicopter over the Island including Ground Zero, where we had been taken on Boxing Day 1958. He visited the Gilbertese village and met the Village school teacher and the District Commissioner. The Prince was then asked to plant a tree to commemorate his visit.

Prince Philip and the School Teacher and school children.

Me after the Guard of Honour.

The next day our Guard of Honour was invited into the village to give the District Commissioner an award, what the award was I can't remember. On the night we were invited once again into the village and the Gilbertese chaps and girls performed their traditional dances for us, dressed in their traditional costumes and they were so proud to perform for us. It was great to see all this, maybe being on the Guard of Honour had its perks after all. I have some photographs of them dancing and I must say all the work we put into bulling our boots and pressing our uniforms was well worth it because we really did look smart, in fact I felt very proud to be British.

The Gilbertese dancing for us.

Chapter 8

ON LEAVE

Ronnie Seddon and I applied for a week's leave in Honolulu which was granted, so we saved up some money to take with us. The day came for us to go and we made our way to the airfield where it had been arranged for us to get a lift on an RAF Hastings aircraft to Honolulu, which was 1,400 miles away. It didn't cost us anything for the travel, we just hitched a free ride with the RAF who travelled to Honolulu on a regular basis to collect the mail and supplies. Several hours later we landed at Hickam Air Base which was an American Air Force Base and our crew told us the day and time that they would pick us up the following week. The American guards on the main gate told us which bus to catch into town, where we were staying at the YMCA (there was no sign of any cowboys, indians, policemen or builders in hard hats). The YMCA catered for service men, particularly the American service men.

Having checked in at the YMCA one of the first things we did was to go down town and buy some civilian clothes, we didn't need much because of the heat. We bought ourselves some lightweight trousers and an Hawaiian shirt, so we were able to change out of our uniforms.

We were in Hawaii when they made it the 50th state of America in 1959, I seem to remember it being in their local papers. It was a great place. We went swimming off Waikiki Beach, we rented surf boards and went surfing in the waves, not as easy as it looks. In the distance was Diamond Head which was the result of a volcanic eruption and is reputed to be 400,000 plus years old. The local people call it Le'ahi but the English name came from British Sailors in the 19th century who thought some crystals they found on a beach were diamonds, hence the name Diamond Head. We visited the Honolulu Zoo, we also went to the International Market Place another great place that's worth a visit.

One night Ronnie and I went drinking in China Town, we were drinking a beer called Pride of the Islands which was a bit potent. We were sitting on high stools in a bar when Ronnie said, 'This beer is like drinking pop.' A few minutes later Ronnie said, 'I'm just off to the toilet,' he got off his stool and fell flat on his face, legless. So, I picked him up and carried him back to the YMCA which thankfully wasn't too far away. Having got him back to our room, I tucked him into his bed, I then got into my bed and went to sleep. The next thing I remember was being woken up by a black guy, he was holding up a soaking wet Ronnie and he asked, 'Is this your buddy?' I said, 'Yes, what's happened to him?' Apparently, Ron had got up to go to the toilet, he had gone down the corridor to the toilets and in his drunken stupor he had gone into one of the showers, switched it on and sat down in the tray. How the chap knew what room to bring him to was because Ron had got the room key in his hand and on the key fob was our room number. This black lad was an American serviceman who was also staying at the YMCA. He helped me dry Ron off and get him into bed, which was good of him. We had a laugh about it, I thanked him for his help, we shook hands and away he went.

The following night Ronnie was still in bed trying to recover from the night before and I was watching a boxing match on the TV between a British boxer called Brian London and an American called Floyd Patterson. I was sitting on a long settee like they have in hotels, with some Americans from Pearl Harbour and we were all watching the boxing. I was shouting for our chap and the Yanks were shouting for their man. As I was the only Englishman there, there was a lot of friendly banter going on and in the end the American beat our chap. Afterwards the Yanks kept buying me drinks, another drunken night.

Ronnie badly wanted a tattoo of a native girl leaning on a palm tree tattooed on his arm. So one night, on our way back from China Town, we passed a tin shack advertising tattooing and Ron made a dash for this shack. There was this little old Polynesian fellow sitting there, Ron told him what he wanted and this old chap got to work. I must admit he did make a good job of it and Ron was over the moon. Ron said 'Come on Brummie have one done.' By the way all the guys called me Brummie or Brum, it's the way it was in the army because of our accents. So, against my better judgement, I ended up having an eagle tattooed on my arm, which I've regretted ever since. It cost me three dollars. No wonder the little old man stayed open late because when the lads were going back to their hotels after having a few drinks, that's when they were most likely to do daft things, whatever nationality they are, like us pair of barmy buggers.

Another night at the YMCA we were entertained by two Hawaiian guys fighting with swords. They were not trying to kill each other or anything, it was all worked out between them, they really were brilliant. This was followed by a troupe of Hawaiian dancing girls wearing grass skirts. I've got to say they were beautiful, with figures to match, performing these Hula Hula dances. Their grass skirts worked overtime, what a pity I didn't have my lawn mower with me. To see these things on TV or in films is one thing but to see them close up in reality now that's something else. It was the same when the Polynesian girls danced for us on Christmas Island, it's a memory I will always treasure. What you have to remember is that in the 1950s people just didn't get to these exotic places, they only saw them in films.

The most popular place to go for a drink or a meal was The Black Cat, across the road from the YMCA. The American servicemen from Pearl Harbour, Hickam Air Base and Schofield Barracks all ate and drank there because it was the cheapest place in town. One night Ronnie and I were in there having a drink when a fight started between some American sailors and all hell broke loose. Before you could say 'hula, hula' the American Shore Patrol came rushing in, looking very smart in their high boots, lanyards and hats. They came in with batons swinging and it was wallop to the back of the neck of the trouble-makers and down they went, no messing.

We were standing by a Juke Box and at the side was an American sailor who was leaning against the wall listening to the music. It was obvious that he had had a few drinks, but he was causing no trouble at all, if someone had moved the wall he would have fallen over. Up came one of the Shore Patrol guys who smacked him on the back of the neck and he just slid down the wall. I said to Ron, 'Let's get the hell out of here, they don't know who we are,' we were in civvy clothes so we made a hasty retreat. The tune that was playing on the Juke Box was *Kansas City*, so whenever I play that tune I think of that night at The Black Cat all those years ago.

There was a gift shop in Hotel Street called Sammy's Gift Shop where I bought some Oriental pyjamas, also a China tea service which Sammy sent to England for me, to my mother. Sammy gave me a Zippo cigarette lighter and he engraved my name on it, I have since given it to my son Paul for a keepsake. On a point of interest, the Hawaiian Flag has the Union Jack in the corner even though it comes under the USA, the reason being is in recognition of a long association with the British. Even though they killed Captain Cook.

Our week's leave soon came to an end and it was time to pack our things and make our way to Hickam Air Base to catch our lift on the RAF Hastings back to the Island. As promised, they were ready and waiting so we boarded the plane. On a Hastings you sat with your back to the Pilot facing the tail end of the plane. There were only us two on the plane other than the crew and we sat with the mail bags and supplies. We had been flying for a short time and I was looking out of the window, when I saw fluid oozing out of the wing, I said to Ron, 'Look at that.' So I went up to the cockpit and told them what I had seen. The RAF Pilot sent one of the crew to have a look. Straight away he said, 'It's okay lads I know what that is. It's the Americans, they have over filled the fuel tanks in the wings, when we have been flying for a while and used some of the fuel up it will stop.' Well, he proved to be correct but if you think about it aviation fuel is supposed to be highly inflammable, what if a spark from one of the engines had set the fuel on fire, it could have blown us out of the sky.

On our return to the Island it was back to work as usual. Until I had a bit of an accident when I was helping lift a heavy box filled with nuts and bolts off the back of a lorry. The driver yanked the box and it fell on the middle finger of my left hand. The trouble was, around the box was a metal band nailed to the box, today they would use a plastic band, but the metal band was hanging loose and it fell on my finger and cut into it like a knife. I was very lucky it didn't take my finger off. The box fell on to the ground spilling its contents into the coral sand and I dashed off to the Naval Medical Centre with my painful bleeding finger. The Navy Medic injected my finger each side of the bone, which was very painful, he then sewed me up and bandaged my hand which now looked like a boxing glove.

I reported back to our work site, when a Corporal saw me and ordered me to pick up a shovel and start shovelling this concrete. His name was Corporal Lawrence and I tried to explain to him that no way could I hold a shovel. He could see my so-called boxing glove, but he insisted and called me a shirker. That was it, I saw red yet again. I picked up the shovel with my good hand and I chased him, threatening to knock his head off. He ran for his life with me after him. Coming towards us was our troop Sergeant, Sergeant Green, who I might add was a good bloke. Lawrence ran behind him, trying to hide behind him, shouting, 'Put him on a charge Sergeant! He's threatening me.' Sergeant Green shouted, 'Hang on there, what's going on?' I explained to him what the trouble was, then Sergeant said, 'Brummie go over there,' so I did as I was told. When I looked back, I could see the Sergeant telling the Corporal off for being so stupid. The Sergeant came over to me, asked me how my hand was, he then said, 'Come on I'll find you a little job.' He found me a job with a paint brush. Yet again I got away with threatening an NCO (will I never learn?) and Corporal Lawrence kept away from that day on.

That night I had no sleep, my finger was throbbing like mad. First thing next morning I reported sick and when the Medic took the bandage off, the stitches were in the bandage. My finger looked a mess, I had coral poisoning and my finger had gone septic overnight. If coral gets into an open wound it poisons the wound, so I had yet another injection and this time the Medic bent my fingers into the palm of my hand then put sticking plaster round my fingers so I could not open my hand. Then once again he bandaged it up, it was an even bigger boxing glove than before. The idea of bending my fingers into my palm was to close the wound, because he could no longer put stitches in it. I was like this for some time, it did eventually heal up but it has left a scar across my finger.

Another accident I had was when I was concreting a base for a building. I was standing in some wet concrete waiting for another load to come when a chap (who came from Aldridge near Walsall named Derek Charles) came up behind me. He was a big lad, he put his arms round me and twisted me. Well, my foot stayed where it was, but I turned round. I slumped down in the concrete in agony, it was the worst pain I had ever felt and the result was a fractured ankle. Derek didn't do it on purpose, he didn't realise my foot was in the concrete.

There I was in a heap in the concrete and Derek thought I was joking until he saw the sweat rolling down my face, then he realised I was in trouble. He picked me up and carried me to the Navy First Aid Post, where they ex-rayed my ankle and found I had a Potts Fracture. So now they put me onto the back of a Navy Land Rover and took me to the RAF Hospital at main camp. The RAF Medics cleaned me up, gave me an injection, then put a plaster slab down the back of my leg and along the bottom of my foot. By now my leg had turned black from my toes to my knee and was swelling up. After a week the swelling had gone down and an RAF Sergeant took me into what looked like the operating theatre, which turned out to be a tent. He took the old plaster off and then got my foot on his chest, gripped my knee with both hands, and pulled my knee towards him. It was just like breaking it all over again, the idea being to get the foot and ankle into place before putting a plaster cast on my leg so that I could walk. So now I had this plaster cast from my knee to my toes, with my toes sticking out. I was in the hospital for another week before they would let me go. The medic told me to go to the Navy Dock Yard and get a piece of Land Rover tyre nailed on the bottom of the cast. On the bottom of the cast was a half moon wooden piece, that's what the tyre had been nailed to. The reason for the tyre was coral is very abrasive and would wear away the plaster.

Chapter 9

BACK HOME

It had been just over twelve months since we first set foot on the Island and in all that time we never witnessed a nuclear bomb explosion, but I read somewhere that our chromosomes would have been altered due to the radiation hanging around after the large nuclear explosion carried out a couple of months or so before we arrived there. This would apply to anyone who served on Christmas island. We were told we would be leaving soon, so we would be home just before Christmas. Our battle dress uniforms were sent to Honolulu to be cleaned and pressed. We were also issued with long johns underwear which had arms and legs in them, they were issued to us because we were due to fly to Winnipeg in Canada where the weather was expected to be well below zero. I was given a roll of crepe bandage to wrap around my toes to prevent them getting frost bitten. When our uniforms came back, mine was a snug fit due to me putting on a bit of weight and no way could I get long johns on as well.

The day came when we were due to say goodbye to Christmas Island. It was a paradise with that blue sea and the sun, I think the Pacific region has got to be the best in the world for beauty and tranquillity, you need to see it to understand what I mean. We boarded an Eagles Airways DC6 Aircraft, still not a jet. There was another one of our lads, Ray Varty, who also had a broken leg and was wearing a plaster, so we were given special seats with a bit more leg room than some of the other seats. As we took off on our way to Honolulu we waved goodbye to the Island.

We had to refuel at Honolulu, then our next stop was San Francisco, where we stayed for two or three days. We stayed at the King George Hotel on Mason Street, the Wells Fargo Bank was just a short walk away. We went on the cable cars up and down those steep hills that you see in films, we explored the city and we could see Alcatraz, which was a mile away in the bay. We were on a bus going somewhere and when we sat down someone tapped me on my shoulder. I looked around and a woman said, 'You can't sit there.' When I asked why not, she said, 'Those seats are for the black people.' So we had to move to another seat but we were in uniform so she knew we were British and didn't know the rules.

We were on the move again, this time we were bound for Winnipeg in Canada, another 1,500 miles away where the temperature would dramatically change. When we arrived in Winnipeg there was snow on the ground and it was well below

Honolulu Airport, on our way back home, me with my leg in plaster.

zero, something in the region of minus 15 degrees. We had travelled from the Equator so it was a bit of a shock. I had my toes bandaged up and when we got off the plane the ground was so slippery I couldn't stand up, with only one leg. The lads had to carry me and Ray Varty into the terminal, where at least it was warm inside. After the plane had been refuelled it was then sprayed with de-icing fluid. We once again boarded the plane and we were ready for take-off, we were racing down the runway when the take-off had to be aborted. The plane came to a halt and the pilot turned the plane around and went back to the terminal. They said that one of the tachometers had stopped working. Eventually it was fixed and away we went.

Next stop was Newfoundland, another 1,700 miles away, by now we were all veteran flyers (over the years I've flown halfway round the world and never been on a jet!). We landed at Gander Airport in Newfoundland where we refuelled in readiness for our last 1,120 miles back to Blackbush Airport near London. We finally arrived in England, a place we had not seen for over twelve months. We went through customs, I had no trouble but I recollect one of our lads had bought some naughty books on his travels and the customs officer seemed very interested in them. I think the customs took them off him.

We were issued with travel passes and away we went, kit bag and all. I made my way back to Sutton Coldfield and it was great to see my parents again after so long. My mom was so glad to see this very tanned son of hers with his leg in a plaster. My dad didn't show much emotion, I think he kept his feelings to himself. I had four weeks leave which meant I didn't have to report back to Maidstone until way after Christmas.

One of the first jobs I had to do was to see my civvy doctor, I had been wearing this plaster now for eight weeks and I was anxious to get it removed before Christmas. I had brought my x-ray home in my kit bag to show the doctor. He sent me to The Cottage Hospital in Sutton Coldfield and the nurse couldn't do enough for me. I was 22 years of age with a deep tan from months of tropical sun and she was eager to know where I had been and I had great pleasure in telling her of my exploits. I could tell she was impressed, in the 1950s if the average person got as far as France they were lucky.

This nurse was cutting off my plaster and chatting to me, I thought to myself my luck is in here, she's nice and she seems keen. Don't forget we had not had the pleasure of ladies company for over a year, so I decided to ask her out for a date that night. After a struggle she finished cutting off my plaster and she peeled it off to reveal my leg looking like a skeleton's and worst of all it smelt, after eight weeks of sweat and not being able to wash it. The nurse took the plaster away and I was so embarrassed with the state and the smell of my leg that while the nurse was away, I quickly put on a sock and a shoe (which I had taken with me), then I hobbled out of the hospital without anyone seeing me. I know I was silly and I'm sure the nurse would have understood and have cleaned my leg. So, I never did get that date with my pretty little nurse. After a few weeks the muscles in my leg went back to normal and I was able to walk normally. I must say the RAF Medics did a good job on me in spite of the primitive conditions.

Christmas and New Year came and went, then it was time for me to report back to Invicta Lines in Maidstone, Kent. In January 1960 I was made Orderly Corporal with the Sergeant Major Freddie Newman, he was a tough little bugger, we called him Fearless Fred. Orderly Corporal was quite a responsible job, it involved me writing the daily orders, organising the Guard Duty Rota and the Duty NCO rota, I also had to inform the cookhouse how many men to feed each day and how many men to feed in seven days' time. I had to keep check of how many men were on leave, how many men were locked up in the guard room. In addition to all this, I was responsible for collecting and distributing the mail each day.

The Sergeant Major sent me down town one morning for something or other, I was in uniform and as I was walking along a lady's voice said, 'Hello Mike.' So,

I stopped and said 'Hello' back. She smiled and said, 'You don't remember me, do you?' I thought ding dong she's nice. I said smiling, 'I'm so sorry but I don't.' It turned out she was Miss Y, the pretty blonde girl I had taken out a few times before going overseas. She was looking as lovely as ever. It was amazing how we bumped into each other and that she recognised me. So, I arranged to take her out that night and that was to be the start of a romance, more of which will be revealed later.

Meanwhile back at camp, I had been doing the Orderly Corporal's job for some weeks, although I was doing the job well enough I lost the job because of my spelling. Try as I might I could not get the hang of spelling and I'm no better now, I'm just rubbish at it. The Sergeant Major would correct my mistakes to keep me out of trouble, but he had enough to do let alone correct my mistakes. So, it was decided it would be best if they got someone who could spell, in the end they got an ex-grammar school lad to take my place. I had to show him what to do, but he was one those lads you couldn't tell him anything, he thought he knew it all, so I just let him get on with it. I don't think the Sergeant Major liked him too much, with me the Sergeant Major would tell me off and end up laughing about it, we had served in Germany and Christmas Island together, I had even played hockey with him, the new lad had not been anywhere or done anything and had an air of superiority about him.

So now I was made a Regimental Policeman (RP), not to be confused with a Military Policeman (MP), to be an MP you had to be six foot tall and I'm 5 foot 7 inches tall. Being an RP meant you looked after your own Regimental Discipline. By now the RPs had taken over the guard duty on the main gate and one morning about 3am, a really chilly morning, I was on guard at the main gate and I was leaning on the back of my sentry box dozing off, when I was aware of someone in front of me. I opened my eyes and there stood an Officer, thinking very quickly, I crossed myself and said, 'Amen. Just a little prayer, Sir,' and I saluted him. He said, 'Well done Sapper, carry on' and then he walked away (joke). One thing you don't do is fall asleep on guard.

Being an RP was not a job I liked. If you had a prisoner, their boot laces were taken off them, also their neck ties and belts, they had nothing that they could harm themselves with. The prisoners had a cell and would have to sleep on a wooden base with a blanket. They would be allowed two cigarettes a day and they had to smoke them standing on a white line as long as the cigarette lasted. One of my jobs was to escort a prisoner, sometimes two prisoners, to the cookhouse for their meals. We marched them briskly in front of us left, right, left, right and we were supposed to kick their heels but I was not like that, I just marched them normally unless there was an officer coming towards us. Then I would say to them 'Officer coming' and we would then quicken up the pace and salute him, then back to normal. At the end of the day these guys were not criminals, they were unlucky, they may have been late coming back off leave or got a bit drunk or upset an NCO or something minor that landed them in the Nick. Look at me for instance, I could have easily been thrown in the Nick more than once. There was one perk of being an RP, if you had a prisoner you could go to the front of the queue at the cookhouse.

I was seeing Miss Y most nights when I was off duty and things were getting rather romantic. I think the trouble was that for over twelve months I had not had the pleasure of a young lady's company and it was very easy to fall for the first girl that came along. Having said that, she was a nice pretty girl. I was due for demob which was going to be a problem for us, she was in Maidstone and I would be in Sutton Coldfield.

I continued as an RP until I was demobbed, I had served just over two years, and it was time to hand back my kit, but we were allowed to keep some kit like towels, underwear and boots. So, I said goodbye to my Army life. Did I enjoy my time in the Army? Yes, I did and I would not have missed it for the world. It has been the grounding for the rest of my life and I am proud to have been a Royal Engineer.

Chapter 10

BACK TO CIVVY STREET

After being demobbed I was due to go back to work at the GEC but not straight away. My cousin Percy, who had his own engineering business called Darlaston Light Engineering, gave me a job as a welder. I had been to a welding school when I was an apprentice, so I could do the job. I was very grateful to Percy because it helped me out financially. When I did get back to the GEC I found it so very hard to settle down, after all the places I had been to, and all the things I had done over the last two years.

Michael Poutney was demobbed before me and he had met a young lady in the summer of 1959, when he was on leave, having just got back from Singapore. The young lady in question was Brenda Godfrey, who I mentioned earlier, the girl I was at school with. When she found out that I was Michael's best friend she nearly had a fit, I think she thought I was a bit of a ruffian. However, when she got to know me a bit better, she realised I wasn't that bad after all and we have become dear lifelong friends right up to this day and speak to each other over the telephone regularly, but more about Brenda later. With Michael courting Brenda I was seeing less of him, which was understandable.

I ran into Miss X, the young dark haired girl that I courted before going into the Army, she was looking great and she told me she was married and her husband was away. When I looked into her eyes, I could see the old spark was still there and she intimated that she would like me to take her out while her husband was away. I can tell you I was very tempted.

While I was away Dad had bought me an old 1940s Morris Minor Post Office Van. Dad had taken the engine out and reconditioned it, he was brilliant with engines. I did the bodywork and I replaced the wooden floor boards. When we put the engine back in and got it started it ran as smoothly as a sewing machine, it was a cracking little van, in fact I passed my driving test first time in it. I said to the Examiner, 'I'm feeling a bit nervous.' He said, 'I thought you were, when I saw you get into the back seat of the van.' Then he said, 'What's the most common road sign?' I said, 'Pick your own Strawberries.' (Joke). Anyway, I passed first time.

I had been saving a bit of money to buy a drum kit, so I went to George Clay's music shop in Broad Street, Birmingham. A guy called Cecil Viles sold me a nice Marine Pearl Premier drum kit, the price was £83, a bit different from today's prices. Cecil Viles played trumpet and I played in the same big band as Cecil back in the 1960s. So now I had a decent drum kit and I was practising like mad. I could now afford a drum teacher. My teacher was Norman Allan, he ran his own band and his wife June sang with the band. I was also learning to read music as well as practising every chance I had. By chance I met another drummer, Jimmy McDonald, who also worked at GEC. Jimmy got me a few gigs and from those gigs came more gigs and in no time at all I was working regularly.

Back to the romance. I was writing to Miss Y in Maidstone and some weekends she would come up to Sutton Coldfield on the train to stay for the weekend and sometimes I would go down to Maidstone, if I wasn't drumming. To cut a long story short, when she came to Sutton, she didn't like me playing the drums, because she had to sit on her own which I understood. It does take a special woman to marry a musician. Having said all that we decided to get engaged and arranged to have the engagement party in Maidstone. After a while I got to thinking, maybe I'm rushing into things, she's not too keen on me playing drums and I have not had much time to sow my wild oats. We sow our wild oats on a Saturday night and pray for a crop failure on Sunday. To be honest I had been going out with other girls that I had met on gigs, so I hadn't been very loyal. When it was time for me to go down to Maidstone to the party, I never turned up.

A few days later a letter turned up asking what had happened, had I been ill? She said she had all the food prepared and she had invited her friends and I hadn't turned up. I didn't answer the letter and we were not on the telephone in those days, thank goodness. Another few days and another letter came, but this time it was a bit stronger, calling me all the names under the sun. I didn't answer that letter either. A third letter came, now this one was really steaming and she told me she was coming up to Sutton with her brothers to sort me out. So once again I got to thinking, if she and her brothers were coming to sort me out, it would be on a weekend so they didn't lose any work. I spoke to a mate of mine, Brian Jones (who had served in the RAF, also on Christmas Island), I explained the situation to Brian and I asked him if he fancied going over to France for the weekend, to get out of the way. Brian agreed, but it caused a break-up with his then girlfriend, this was a blessing in disguise because he ended up marrying a far better girl and that's his wife Heather.

The weekend came and we motored down to Southend Airport in Brian's Morris Minor, it was a nice car. We boarded a twin-engine Bristol Freighter Aircraft and flew to Calais Airport where we got a coach into the town. We spent the day visiting one or two bars, I can't remember what we were drinking, but we did have a nice day. We flew back to Southend on another Bristol Freighter, where we collected Brian's Morris Minor. If I remember correctly we slept in the car. When I got back home, I asked my dad if anyone had turned up, he said no one had been. I didn't get any more letters and I decided to face the music if they did turn up. Well, nobody ever did come to see me. I'm not proud of the way I handled things, she didn't deserve the humiliation she must have gone through. I really hope she found some nice guy, who treated her properly.

I once had a girlfriend called Bubbles, I called her Bubbles because she never wiped her nose, she had a lovely set of teeth, she only needed a white tooth and she would have had a snooker set.

Chapter 11

MARRIED LIFE

It was 1961 and a year had passed since I was demobbed from the Army. I was still finding it hard to settle down and all my old mates were getting married. Michael and Brenda had married and moved down to Tadley in Basingstoke, Michael had secured a job at the Atomic Weapons Establishment in Aldermaston. So, I didn't see much of him now.

I had a lot of girlfriends but none that lasted, my dad said to me after the Maidstone affair, you want to see how many girlfriends you can get in a week, I didn't need telling twice. When I look back on what he was telling me, I can see what he was trying to say, sooner or later you will know when you find the right one. Not that I was looking to get married, that didn't enter my head, I was just having a good time. So, you could say I had my fair share of lady friends.

I had one Saturday night off and with another chap I had made friends with at work, Phil Arnold, we decided to go to a dance at the Assembly Rooms in Tamworth. There we were eyeing up the girls when Phil said, 'Mike, see those two girls over there? I fancy the one on the right and I'm going to ask her for a dance, you ask her mate.' So, I asked this very slim young lady to dance, to be honest I had got the best one. We were dancing and she said her name was Eileen. I thought, I'll impress her with my dancing, I said to her, 'Dancing is in my blood.' Eileen said, 'You must have poor circulation, it's not reached your feet yet.' The four of us spent a pleasant night dancing and having a drink together.

After the last dance, Phil and I took the girls home in my Morris Minor Post Office Van, to Polesworth not far from Tamworth. I arranged to see Eileen the following night, we went to the cinema in Tamworth and the film we saw was *North to Alaska*. Our second date was the four of us at one of my gigs at The

Golden Cross Pub in Aston, Birmingham. It was the first time I had put a band together under my own name The Mike Rubery Trio.

Eileen and I clicked right from the first time we met and we started seeing a lot of each other. One of the stories Eileen used to tell was the first time I picked her up from her house her mother saw me from a short distance and said to Eileen, 'Don't you get bringing any foreigners here.' Eileen said, 'Mom, he is not a foreigner, he's been overseas in the Army.' Even twelve months later I still had my tropical tan and that story has become a family joke.

All four of us sometimes went out together, then Phil and his lady split up, but Eileen and I stayed together. Eileen would come with me on gigs, usually on Saturday nights, when she didn't have go to work the next day. Eileen was a tailoress, making men's suits for a firm called Bradleys, who had a workshop in Tamworth. Eileen would sit in the wings of the stage, with two knitting needles and a ball of wool, knitting away while I would be playing in the band on stage. It never bothered Eileen that I was a drummer, she didn't mind at all. When I started playing in regular bands, she got to know the other wives and girlfriends of the other band members and we all became friends.

In the early days I played for a lot of weddings and on one such occasion I was playing in a bit of a rough pub in Birmingham and at the end of the evening it was discovered that someone had stolen the top tier of the wedding cake. As I had round drum cases, I became the prime suspect and was surrounded by the bride and groom with their family, who by now had had a few drinks and were in an ugly mood looking for the missing cake. I was ordered in no uncertain terms to open my cases for them to check. Needless to say, they found nothing in my cases but I couldn't get out of the place fast enough.

Another night we were playing at a club in Birmingham and my mom and dad, Eileen, Michael Poutney, Brenda, Brenda's sister and some friends of ours had all come to see us play. At the end of the night, we packed the drums away and loaded my van when someone suggested stopping at a chippy for some fish and chips. So, on the way home we stopped at a chippy and were standing in the queue when two yobs, eating their chips, started using bad language and I mean really bad language. I felt embarrassed because I had my mother and the other ladies in our little group, other people in the queue were also whispering to each other about the language. So, I went up to these yobs and asked them to moderate their language because there were ladies present. The one yob, who had a tattoo around his neck and was the one with the biggest mouth, threw his chip paper at me. Once again I lost my cool and I hit him, he bounced off the shop window and came out with even more language complaining I had hit him. My dad tried to calm things down, but it was too late. Outside we went, which was fine by me, I was fired up by now. Having got outside we suddenly found two more of his mates out there so now there was four of them and only me and my dad. Michael had taken our ladies off out of harm's way. Three of the yobs had a go at my dad, two of them, one each side holding his arms and the one who I had hit was ready to plough into him. Before I could get there to help him, Dad had taken a step forward then a step back and banged these two yobs' heads together. Then Dad grabbed the pullover off the yob in front of him, hit him and laid him out.

It was all James Bond stuff. It now went quiet. Dad said, 'Let's get in the cars and go,' so Eileen and I climbed in the van ready to drive off, when the fourth yob, who we had forgotten about, came from nowhere and kicked the passenger door. Now that was it, I saw red again. I got out and I grabbed a starting handle from behind my seat and dashed round the van ready to part the yob's hair with it, only to find Eileen on top of him with her hands round his throat strangling him. She had jumped out of the van and taken him by surprise, he didn't expect a woman to have a go. Thinking about it, it was just as well Eileen did get there first because I may have fractured his skull. Within seconds of this happening, blue lights and sirens came racing up the road, the cavalry had arrived. The chip shop owner had phoned the police and the yobs legged it in all directions. We told the police what had happened and they went off looking for them, but there was no chance of catching them.

In no time at all I knew that this slim attractive girl was the one for me. One night when I had taken her home, we were leaning up against the toilet wall, when I asked her to marry me. We then heard the toilet flush, not realising her dad was in there. Very romantic don't you think? We got engaged on the 16th December 1961, I was playing at the Imperial Hotel in Birmingham. Eileen went out with my mom and dad for the night and I met up with them after my gig.

We were courting for three years, when one day my mom told us that she had heard that a bedsitter was going for rent at The Keep on Weeford Road. The Keep was owned by Walter Smith the butcher and Mrs Smith, Walter Smith's widow, rented a couple of bedsits so we ended up renting one of them. We had a room with a sofa which folded out into a bed, it sagged in the middle, which I might add brought us closer together. It was only a small room, when you opened the door the doorknob got into bed with you. We shared a bathroom with another young couple who rented the other bedsitter. It was a very big house with a central staircase leading off to both sides of the house and underneath the house was a large cellar.

So now all we had to do was get married. We quickly got our marriage arrangements sorted and within a few weeks we were married on the 3rd October

The happy couple.

1964 at Polesworth Abbey Church. It was a small but lovely wedding, the day was really nice, the sun was shining and it was really warm. When we came back from our honeymoon, having paid for the wedding, food, drinks, the honeymoon and rent in advance, all we had to our name was a Ford Anglia Van, a kit of drums and half a crown (ten and a half pence in today's money) but we didn't care, we were happy.

On to 1967, which was a bit of a momentous year. I was made redundant from the GEC, but within a week I had found another job at Press Steel Fishers in Castle Bromwich, Birmingham (which is now the Jaguar Land Rover works). I had been working there just a few weeks when I started playing in Fishers Brass Band. The Musical Director was John Bright and he was happy with me even though I wasn't a brass band type of drummer, to me the music just didn't swing. I did have some fun in that band though, to end the night they used to give me a drum solo where the band would walk off stage leaving me to play for five minutes, then two of them would come back on stage wearing white coats and start taking the drum kit away a bit at a time until I was left with just a snare drum. The parting shot was to come and carry me off, kicking and screaming, usually accompanied by a round of applause.

The other thing that happened in 1967 was I met a keyboard player, his name was John Speak he was a very good player and I learnt a lot from him. It was John who got me into playing for cabaret, a different style of drumming, with tempos like 2/4, tempos that never seemed to be played in dance bands. Although I did not know it at the time, it was through John that my life was due to change.

We had been living at The Keep for a few months when we had the chance to rent a small cottage in Slade Lane, just down the road from the Keep, and 400 yards across the field from the cottage where I was born. We rented this cottage and lived there for four years. It was during this time that we had been trying for a family, we had been trying for some time with no luck, but we had a lot of fun trying. Then we went on holiday to the Norfolk Broads on a boat and we think that while we were on this boat we clicked. So, you can see we got our son the hard way standing up in a hammock. Our son, Paul Michael Rubery, was born on the 18th January 1968 in Good Hope Maternity Hospital.

I remember being in the waiting room, nervously waiting for Paul to put in an appearance, when a nurse called me into the delivery room to see Eileen and Paul. I was so pleased to see Eileen and that she was okay. The nurse gave me Paul to hold, it was quite an emotional moment, seeing and saying hello to your son for the first time. I looked at him and I had a tear in my eye, I would have known him anywhere, if he had been amongst six babies I would have been able to pick him out. I used to visit Eileen and Paul every night on my way to my nightly gig. They were in hospital for a week. When we got home, I found it scary that we had this little bundle of life to look after. I found the responsibility frightening, but Eileen took it all in her stride.

When I would get home at night after my gig, I had three things to do: No.1 unload my drums; No.2 take our Labrador dog Benny for a walk down the lane and No.3 change Paul's nappy and clean him up. This enabled Eileen to get a good night's sleep. To be fair Paul would sleep through the night, I only remember having one night when he kept us awake, so we were very lucky.

On the 30th of May 1968 John Speak and I were booked to play at Walsall Town Hall and top of the bill was The Karl Denver Trio. After the show the agent asked John, 'How much do I owe your drummer?' John

My little family.

came over to me and asked, 'The agent wants to know how much do you want for the gig?' I replied, '£5.' Later John came back with my £5 and told me the agent had said that he could not afford me. So, I thought to myself, that's done it, I've overpriced myself, £5 was good pay for a gig in 1968. I didn't think the agent would book me again, but how wrong I was. The agent was Bernard Parr and he started booking us for shows such as the David Whitfield Show and Ruby Murray. We also worked with a drag act called Billy Breen who later became known as Larry Grayson.

In 1969/70 the cottages where I was born came up for sale as Birmingham City Council was selling them off and they were offered to my parents as sitting tenants. Dad didn't want to buy them, so he suggested to the Council that I could buy them, being a Canwell lad and also being born there. Birmingham Council agreed but I had to buy the two cottages which was okay by me. By now I was working six or seven days a week in the factory and drumming most nights of the week, in fact I was working my heart out to get money for my little family.

So, we bought the two cottages. My mom and dad were still living in one cottage and the other cottage was derelict with no electricity, running water or toilet, nothing at all. We set to and had it modernised, we had a septic tank installed in the garden to accommodate the toilets and when the cottage was finished we moved Mom and Dad into it. Now they had a proper kitchen, a bathroom and a toilet, no longer did they have to go 25 yards down the garden to the toilet and they loved all these new amenities. We then set about bringing the

Our cottages.

other cottage up to the same standard and then we moved in next door, the place where I was born. While all this was going on we were paying to rent where we lived and the mortgage on the cottages, but it was all worthwhile in the end.

One of the regular gigs I had was playing for striptease artists. One day I was loading up my drums, when my dad came across the yard and asked me if I was still playing for those strippers. I said yes. He said, 'I've never seen a stripper.' I said, 'Come with me, you can help carry my drums.' Dad asked, 'Can we take my friend George with us so I'm not on my own?' So he phoned his mate and we arranged to pick him up.

Usually there was a comedian and two strippers but on this occasion there was just one stripper and she was a smashing black girl, full of fun and with a great figure. I always seemed to be the fall guy for these strippers, they would hang their bras and panties on my cymbals. This time the girl removed her bra and put it on my head, so it looked like a pair of horns. In those days when a stripper had finished her act, she had to strike a pose and then keep still until the curtains were drawn. This girl had struck her pose and the compere then turned this big wheel to close the curtains, she then came over to me laughing to retrieve her bra from my head. She then put her hand at the back of my neck and pulled my face into her boobs and wobbled them in my face, it was like having your face slapped. For some unknown reason the compere turned his big wheel and opened the curtains to reveal the scene and a voice from the audience shouted, 'You dirty

Ruby Murray.

little bugger!' It was my dad. So, as you can see being a drummer did have its perks.

The first time I met Ruby Murray was at John Speak's house. We were working with Ruby that evening and running through her music. Ruby had her little boy Timothy with her so I gave him a pair of my drum sticks and being a little lad he was over the moon with his sticks. Ruby never forgot this and every time we worked together she would remind me of the sticks. Timothy became a singer himself, but sadly died in 2020 at the age of 55 with heart problems.

I visited Ruby's house in Northampton-shire a couple of times, she was one of my all-time favourites. She was a very feminine lady with a lovely warm personality. Ruby made musical history by having five hit records in the Top Twenty Charts in one week. Her birthday was 29th March, the day after mine, but she was two years older than me. She married Bernie Burgess who sang in the Jones Boys singing group and at one time he ran the Cresta Club in Solihull. I remember playing for the Jones Boys in a hotel in Gloucester once, but Bernie wasn't with them at that time.

Ruby Murray was always good with musicians and so was David Whitfield the great male tenor vocalist. He was the first British artist to not only have a number 1 single in the UK, but also in America with his big hit *Cara Mia*. When David was on stage he commanded it, he had stage craft and charisma, so it came naturally to him. I had a lot of laughs with David, he liked to have a drink and tell a few funny stories.

I remember taking my dad with me one night to Madeley Hall in Telford, Dad loved David's singing and he wanted to see him. Being a good distance away we started out early. I was putting my drums up when in walked David and I introduced him to my dad, who was excited as he had never really met anybody well-known before. Dad said,

David Whitfield.

'Hello David, I remember you when you were good.' I couldn't believe what I was hearing. What Dad was really trying to say was that he remember him when he was in the Hit Parade! David knew what he meant and laughed his socks off. The place had a snooker room downstairs and David took Dad off to play snooker until it was time for David to get changed into his suit and perform his act. Dad had a great night and it was something he could tell his mates about at work.

I have another story about David and his snooker. We were in a show and David was, as usual, top of the bill. Also on the show were some dear friends of mine, Linda and Martin Barry, a very polished act who I always enjoyed working with. During the first half of the show David was playing snooker in another room, every now and then he would pop into the foyer and peep through the door into the showroom to see how far into the show they were so he could judge the time to go into the dressing room and get changed. An old chap who was the doorman checking people's tickets saw David do this several times, so when the time did come for David to go up to the dressing room, the old chap on the door

65

said, 'Hey you, I've been watching you and you're trying to get in without paying.' David explained who he was, but the doorman wouldn't let him in. So, David went outside and up to the dressing room window and knocked on it, Martin Barry opened the window and pulled David through. I would have loved to have seen the doorman's face when he saw David on stage.

Yet another story about working on the David Whitfield Show. On the show were some more friends of mine, The Lyntones another very good act, and Keith Gordon who was a clarinet player. Keith would finish the first half of the show with a Benny Goodman and Gene Krupa feature, with clarinet and drum solo. On this particular night we had finished the first half with the drum solo and we were all in the dressing room. I was washing my hands and face after sweating with the drum solo, when suddenly the door burst open and in came this woman with big boobs and a big hairstyle to match shouting, 'Where is he? He's lovely.' Well, we all thought she was referring to David, I turned around from the wash basin and she saw me and yelled, 'There he is!' and made a lunge for me. In doing so her false teeth shot out of her mouth onto the floor, I was horrified. But the funniest part was when Tony of The Lyntones, Keith Gordon and David Whitfield pretended to stamp on her teeth. The poor woman went red in the face, grabbed her teeth and shot out of the door. You have no idea how relieved I was and of course it was the big laugh for the rest of the week.

David came to our cottage a couple of times when we were working locally, and after the show it would be back to the Ruberys'. I would ring Eileen to warn her that some of the show were coming back, Eileen would pop next door and tell Mom and Dad so they would stay up to see everybody. Eileen would make a load of sandwiches and David would put the kettle on and make the tea, he was a down to earth guy. David would also go next door and say hello to my mom and dad. The last time I saw David was when two of our dear friends, Bob and Wendy Levy, told us that David was appearing at their club. I told them I knew him, so they got four tickets for us to go and see him. After the show I went up to his dressing room to see him, there was a queue of his fans waiting to get his autograph, when I walked in he jumped up and said, 'Mike how are you? Where's Eileen?' I said, 'She's out front with some friends.' He left the autograph hunters and walked into the room and called Eileen and our friends up to the dressing room. He made a big fuss of us all and told us he was off on a tour of Australia with the David Whitfield Show. A few weeks later, while in Australia, he suffered a brain haemorrhage and very sadly died, he was only 54 years of age.

Another man I had a lot of time for was Bert Weedon OBE. He was the author of the Guitar book called *Play in a Day* which was hugely successful. A lot of great guitar stars like Pete Townsend, George Harrison and Eric Clapton, to name but a few, all learnt to play guitar from reading Bert's book. I worked with Bert many times and I got to know his wife Maggie and his son Lionel. Bert played guitar on many of the rock and roll stars' records, people like Adam Faith, Tommy Steele and many more. He even played for Frank Sinatra, Nat King Cole and all the big bands of the day. Bert had a big hit with *Guitar Boogie Shuffle* which he played every night in his act.

Bert collected silver spoons and when he found out that I made a lot of the props for the shows and pantomimes I worked on, he asked me if I could make him a cabinet to

Bert Weedon.

display his silver spoons. I made him a cabinet with Queen Ann legs, glass sides and a glass top. Eileen finished it off by putting red velvet in the bottom of the cabinet so the silver spoons could be displayed on velvet. Bert came round to our cottage to collect it and he was over the moon with it, he asked me if I would make another one but I never did get around to it.

I used to chat to Bert and one night we were working in a club in Portsmouth, we were in the dressing room and Bert was cleaning his guitar. I had a piece of drum music with a funky rhythm written down and I was trying to work it out. Bert asked, 'What you got there, Mike? Let's have a look.' Bert could read music so when he looked at it, he understood it. He said, 'Mike I'll tell you what to do, put words to the notes.' And this was what he came up with, 'Come to church for coffee and sandwiches.' It worked, I was able to play it in no time and I never forgot that little trick, I have used it many times with different words to fit different rhythms. Bert was a gentleman and when I saw on TV that Bert had passed away I rang his wife Maggie and offered my condolences. Poor Maggie was very tearful, but she did tell me they had still got the cabinet.

Another nice guy I worked with was Bob Monkhouse OBE, he was another gentleman. I worked with Bob a few times and he was the only comic to ask us if we minded if he took the mickey out of us on stage. We had no objections, we were used to the comics taking the mickey out of us, it was all in good fun. Every night we worked with Bob he would send Jackie, his wife, up to the bar to buy us a drink. Bob was a very clever comic and he had an amazing memory.

It was in the 1960s when John Speak and I were on a show in Bilston with a lady vocalist called Jackie and another old friend of ours Del Derrick, who was a great entertainer. To complete the line-up was a comic called Benny Nightingale, who was a black chap that we had worked with many times before. We had the gear all set up when in came a committee man, having seen Benny, he said, 'Is he with you lot?' We said, 'Yes, he's our comic.' The committee man said, 'He can't come in here, we have a colour ban in this club.' 'But he's in the show.' 'I don't care, he's not coming in.' Del Derrick took charge of the situation and said, 'We don't have a colour ban in showbusiness, if Benny doesn't perform, none of us will perform.' With that we packed-up our gear and put it all back into the cars.

By now the club was full, the people had paid their money and were waiting to be entertained. The committee man came to us, panicking, and said, 'We have had a quick meeting and have decided to let the comic perform.' The show was back on, all the gear had to be unloaded from our cars and quickly set up, then away we went. When it was time for Benny to grace the stage, his first words were, 'Ladies and Gentlemen, do you remember when you were little kids and your mother would say if you don't behave the Bogeyman will come and get you? Well, here I am!' The audience just fell about laughing and the show was a success.

One of the bands I was playing in was The Dave Rollinson Big Band. One night we were playing at the Scraptoft College in Leicester and top of the bill were the Spencer Davis Group, a very well-known Birmingham outfit who had a few hits under their belts. Also on the show was a chap who pushed nails through his nose and ate razor blades. I had taken Eileen with me on this particular night and poor Eileen couldn't bear to watch this chap with his razor blades, if he'd coughed he was in danger of castrating himself.

I played at the De Montfort Hall in Leicester, once again with The Dave Rollinson Big Band, we were playing for general dancing and they also had a cabaret, this time it was The Morton Fraser Harmonica Gang. Top of the bill were Peter Eccleston and Brenda Winslade, who at that time were the World Champion Ballroom Dancers. We had no rehearsal, the music was just handed out to our 15-piece band and when they danced they went from one tempo to another without stopping. You had to read your music and make sure you didn't lose your place otherwise you missed the tempo changes. It could be a bit hair-raising but everything went well and we all played the music correctly, so the dancers were happy.

Appearing with The Billy Fury Show, now that's a night I won't forget in a hurry. John Speak and I were booked to play on the Show in Birmingham. We got set up and we were all ready to start, Billy had his own band and they, like us, were also all set up. John and I opened the show and played for the acts on the first half then Billy

Billy Fury.

Fury was then due to play the whole of the second half. But come the time for Billy to do his bit there was no sign of him anywhere, so something had to done. We went on again with the first half acts to keep the show going until Billy turned up but it wasn't till about 11.30pm when Billy finally turned up.

The room was packed out with money paying customers, who by now were in an irate state to say the least. Two committee men came on stage and the one said, 'Quick let's get Billy Fury on,' and the other one said, 'No, he's too late,' and pressed the button to close the curtains. The other committee man said, 'Yes, he's going on,' and pressed the button and the curtains opened again. Then the two committee men started fighting on the stage in full view of the audience. Within seconds the whole of the club was in uproar, there were bottles and glasses being thrown and fighting had broken out. I was trying to get my drums off the stage and into the dressing room out of harm's way. I barricaded the door for the safety of my drums and of course myself.

The dressing room I was in was on the opposite side of the stage to where Billy was, I was busy getting my drums into their cases when Billy came running across the stage to where I was. He looked like he'd been crying, I was told later that someone had hit him. Anyway, he was about to jump through the window when I pulled him back (the back of the club was built on stilts so the dressing rooms were about 25 foot off the ground with our cars parked underneath). I explained the danger to Billy and then I unblocked the door and peeped out, they were still fighting over the other side of the club. I opened the fire escape door which led down to the ground and let Billy out, he was gone like a shot. I then blocked myself back in again until everything had died down. When I did venture out of the dressing room into the big room it was in a terrible state, I would not fancy clearing it up. I suppose you could say that I saved Billy Fury from an early grave or show business would have lost one of its brightest stars before their time. The sad thing was nobody got paid. I worked with Billy a couple of times afterwards down in the south of England and he was never late again.

We were on a show in Handsworth, Birmingham when top of the bill was a chap called Yodelling Bill Gore who had appeared on the smash hit TV show

Opportunity Knocks. Bill had won no less than five times on that show and his act consisted of him being dressed in Lederhosen and wearing boots decorated in ultraviolet paint. These boots had bump and go motors inside them and would travel across the stage illuminated by two ultraviolet fluorescent tubes. All of this was accompanied by Bill's expert yodelling. It was a unique act, there was nothing quite like it on the cabaret scene. I will say this as a drummer, Bill was a shock to the system because of the speed he took off into his first number, it took me by surprise and I'm sure this had been the experience of other drummers. Bill launched into this ultra fast 2/4 tempo, not to worry I did keep up with him. Over the years Bill and his family and my family became friends.

Bernard Parr, my agent, devised a show called Stars in Your Eyes and I was asked to be the drummer with John Speak. The show included a male dancer and four dancing girls that went under the name of Barry Young and Les Girls, also an old mate of ours Del Derrick, plus a couple of other acts. Within the show we had comedy sketches, of which I was asked to play small parts, as well as play the drums. Over the years Stars in Your Eyes became very well-known and I spent ten happy years in that show. I will tell you more about it later.

Early years of Stars in Your Eyes, I'm on the far right.

I must remind you that while I was working on these shows in and around the Midlands, I was getting home in the early hours and then next morning getting up and going to work in the factory. It was while I was playing in Wrexham, on the Stan Stennett show, that Stan offered me a job playing drums in his summer shows and pantomimes. You may remember Stan being in the *Black and White Minstrel Show* on TV, he played Sid Hooper in the soap opera *Crossroads* and was also in *Coronation Street* and many other TV programmes. I told him I would have to think about it and it planted a seed in my head.

Two things then happened. One was John Speak went off to Canada with David Whitfield, as his Musical Director. So, Bernard Parr teamed me up with a guy who took over from John Speak, a keyboard player called Billy Pearce and we hit it off musically and we also became mates. The second thing was I was put on night shift at the factory, which of course, interfered with my music. I hated this night shift lark, plus the fact in the 1960s the unions in the car factories were forever calling strikes, if you stirred your tea the wrong way round it was a good reason to call a strike. I asked Eileen how she felt about me giving up working in the factory and doing my drumming full time, Eileen replied, 'You love your drumming and if you think you can make a living at it, I will stand by you come what may.' So, I decided to leave the factory and to be honest I never looked back. The guys I worked with bought me a lovely leaving gift, a carrying case to put my clothes in on my forthcoming travels and also a nice bottle of wine to go with it.

Chapter 12

DRUMMING FOR A LIVING

My first pro job, as it were, was a six-week run of Stars in Your Eyes with my new co-pilot Billy Pearce. Would you believe I left the factory on the Friday and the following Sunday night Stars in Your Eyes were booked to play at the factory social club. Some of the chaps I had worked with were in the audience, so I played my heart out that night, of course they had never seen me in my natural musical environment before.

Billy Pearce and myself.

I had accepted Stan Stennett's offer to play for his summer shows and at the end of the six-week run of Stars in Your Eyes we went into summer season at the Floral Hall in Southport. Eileen and I had bought a caravan to live in during the season and we found a caravan site where we did a deal with the owner for a better price regards the rent, due to the fact we were going to be there for a number of weeks. We found Southport to be a nice place, some people said it was an old folk's paradise, having said that, the shop windows were bi-focal.

Back to the show. It was The Stan Stennett Summer Stars with Stan topping the bill, we had a dance troupe called The Ballet Mont Martre, an excellent troupe. Their crowning glory was the *Can Can*, we played it every night and the girls would jump up into the air and land on the floor doing the splits, it was eye-watering to see. Then we had Curry's Dancing Waters, which was situated at the back of the stage and was jets of water that were illuminated by different coloured lights. The water jets would dance up and down to music such as waltz time, it was a very colourful sight.

We also had a guy called Frank Holder who sang and played the conga drums. Frank came from Georgetown in Guyana and he had worked with Johnny Dankworth and Cleo Laine, he also worked with Billy Eckstein and Nat King Cole. In 2015 he was given a Lifetime Achievement Award for his work in jazz.

Next on the show was a lady magician, Paula Lee and Company. Paula's husband and two daughters assisted her in her act, her husband was Roy Lester who was the comedian on the show. Her eldest daughter Claudi eventually married Charlie Cairoli's son Charlie jnr, Charlie Cairoli snr was the clown at Blackpool Tower.

An act called The Falcons were on the show, they were a man and wife team, real old pros who knew the business inside out. They performed a paper hanging scene with wallpaper paste shooting out the top of their bowler hats, it really was hilarious to watch.

Our lady soprano, Lesley King, was a very glamorous queen of song. Lesley had appeared on radio and TV and had also appeared with Max Bygraves on a Royal Command Performance at the Alhambra Theatre in Glasgow.

I have to say, up to that time this was the biggest show I had ever worked on. It was a first-class show and received good reviews in the newspapers. It was normal practice for summer shows such as ours to be welcomed to the town we were working at, so we were invited to the Mayor's Parlour. We put on our best clothes to meet the Mayor of Southport and we all arranged to meet up at the Floral Hall and go to the Parlour together. I was wearing my best suit and was waiting for everyone to turn up, so I sat on one of the radiators to warm my bum. Unbeknown to me, the stage manager had painted the radiator with green paint, so there I was with green paint on the back of my trousers. I quickly found the stage manager and asked him why he had not put a sign on the radiator, he said he did put a sign on but nobody sat on it so he took it off. He dashed off and got some white spirit, I took my trousers off and he proceeded to remove the paint. After he had soaked my trousers in white spirit, which dried quickly, I put my trousers back on but I was left with an over-powering smell of white spirit which seemed to follow me around. We all arrived at the Parlour, we were introduced to the Mayor and when it was my turn Stan Stennett said, 'Mr Mayor this is Mike Rubery our drummer.' Well the Mayor looked at me with suspicion, with the fumes coming off the white spirit I'm sure he thought I was an alcoholic. I did do my best to keep away from any naked flames in case I combusted, have you heard that song *Great Balls of Fire?*

We used to get Sunday nights off when the theatre would stage Sunday night concerts with acts such as Mott The Hoople, The Dubliners, The Spinners or sometimes Wrestling. I used to take Eileen and Paul to see these concerts as I could get free tickets. One upcoming Sunday concert was due to feature Peter Noone and the Hermits, also on the show was Jack Diamond, the comedian who was the warm-up comic for TV's *The Comedians*. At one time Jack was engaged to Julie Goodyear who played Bet Lynch in *Coronation Street*. There was also a little chap called Gerry Monroe who had a few hits like *Sally, It's a Sin to Tell a Lie, My Prayer* and a few more besides. This show was to be backed by the local Musicians Union Representative, who was a keyboard player. In those days as a pro-musician you had to be a member of the Musicians Union and within a week of playing in any theatre an MU Representative would pay you a visit to check your Union Card, if you were not in the union you would not be allowed to work.

Just before this show an MU representative came to see Stan, to ask him if Billy Pearce and I would play for this particular Sunday show, it was up to Stan to say yes or no because we were contracted to him. Stan agreed it was okay with him as long as we were well paid. Everything was agreed which was great for us, it meant an extra night's pay. We later found out that the reason the Union Representative had dropped out of playing for the show was he had heard along the grapevine that Gerry Monroe had once walked off stage because he thought the musicians were not good enough to play for him, so the Representative got cold feet.

The Sunday night arrived and I got Eileen and Paul tickets, the theatre was packed which was always nice to see. We did the show and we had no trouble with Gerry Monroe at all, he sang in a Falsetto voice which was unusual for a man, in fact I enjoyed playing for him. Gerry was a nice guy and the audience loved him. Peter Noone was last on to finish the night and once again the audience loved him. We were all in one big dressing room getting changed when there was banging on the door, it was the autograph hunters. Peter Noone said, 'Make them wait, I'm not ready yet.' When we were all changed, Peter Noone said, 'Okay, I'm ready let them in.' The autograph hunters came in and although they did go to Peter, they also wanted to see Gerry Monroe, I think he stole the show.

Going back to our own show, one of the scenes we did was a Balloon Ballet which consisted of Stan Stennett, Roy Lester and Frank Holder all dressed in tutu skirts. What made it really funny was the fact they had got a big balloon which they had to pass between their legs, it was great and always got a big laugh from the audience. I had to rehearse the sound effects for all this, I had a suitcase full of sound effects and I think I used most of them on this so-called Ballet. All this was performed to the music of *The Dance of the Sugar Plum Fairy.*

Once a week the council ran a Miss Rosebud Competition for little girls aged five or six years of age. They asked Stan if he would be the judge once a week, Stan then asked Billy and I to judge with him. This was done outside and the girls would parade on a purpose-built open air stage. The compere would introduce each little girl and they held a card with a number on it, then we had to pick the little girl we considered the prettiest. We were on a hiding to nothing with the girls' mothers. We would hand the result to the compere, he would then announce the winner and we would then get up out of our seats to leave. The mothers of the girls who had not won would bang their pushchairs into our legs and demand an explanation as to why their daughters had not won. We had bruises all over our legs, but we soon wised up. What we did after that was, when we handed in the result, we beat a quick retreat before the compere announced the winner.

At the end of the season, we packed all the gear, hitched up the caravan and headed for Porthcawl Pavilion Theatre where we took the whole show for one week. One night after the show we were having a drink in the bar, which was situated underneath the stage, I can only describe it as a Beachcomber type of bar. I had not been feeling too well, I had bought Eileen and Paul a drink and they were talking to some of the members of the show. I got myself a pint of beer and sat in a quiet corner on my own. What had happened was my left eye and face had dropped and the left side of my mouth had dropped. I sat there thinking to myself, that's it I've had a stroke this is the end of me. I must have looked awful because Stan Stennett and Roy Lester came across to me, Stan said Roy is going to take you to the doctor in Porthcawl in the morning, so even they were worried about me.

Next morning, Roy came round to our caravan and away we went to see the doctor. When we got to the surgery there were two doctors, as we walked in the one doctor pointed at me and said, 'Bell's palsy.' I thought to myself, oh my God it's worse than a stroke. He then explained that Bell's palsy was a facial paralysis, they don't really know what causes it. Some say it's caused by stress or from cold draughts from windows, there seems to be different causes. It can also run in families, apparently there is a gene that can sometimes show itself and this seems to be what happened to us, as some years later both Eileen and Paul suffered with Bell's palsy. Paul has been left with weak muscles under his left eye which now tends to droop a little. Eileen's cleared up without any trouble, but I have trouble pronouncing the letter P. The doctor gave me some tablets and a letter to give to my own doctor when I got back home at the end of the week.

When I turned up at the theatre on the night to do the show Stan had brought in another drummer from Cardiff, he was standing by just in case I had a stroke, the symptoms are very similar. However, I did my job and walked into our band compound wearing sunglasses, people in the audience must have thought I was a bit of a poser wearing sunglasses inside a dimly lit theatre. The problem was my left eye would not blink and I could not control my lips, when we got to the Balloon Ballet and it was time to use the sound effects, I had to hold my lips together and then blow my whistles.

It was a difficult time for me, but I did manage to do my job for the rest of the week. When we returned home, I went to my own doctor and he continued with the same treatment and things began to

Stan Stennett.

improve, after about six weeks my face was back to normal (I thought it might improve my looks but it didn't).

Having returned home from Porthcawl, we went straight into rehearsals for another four-week run of Stars in Your Eyes and after that Billy Pearce and I were booked to play for the Kaye Sisters for another four weeks in South Wales. We only had to play for the Kayes but we were doubling every night, which meant playing one club and then dashing off to work another club. The club we doubled at was a nightclub in Port Talbot and because we were doubling, Billy and I used to try and borrow the resident musicians' drums and keyboards because it saved a lot of time when we were racing to get to the next club. We were working at The Showboat in the Mumbles off Swansea Bay, it was a great venue and a lot of the stars of the day performed there. On our show was our old friends The Morton Fraser Harmonica Gang and Malcolm Roberts, a vocalist, one of his hits was *Love is All*. And then there were the Kaye Sisters who had a few hits of their own, such as *Paper Roses* and others with Frankie Vaughan.

The Showboat's stage was built in the shape of a ship's bow, hence the name The Showboat, it was 4 foot high and surrounded by water which was about 18 inches deep. On the other side of the water was the cabaret floor where the acts performed and the drums were sited at the front of the stage, being the bows.

During the show, the Kaye Sisters would pick up some guy's pint of beer and all three of them would have a sip and then hand it to me, I would then drink it up without stopping, usually to a round of applause.

On one particular night the guy whose drink it was got upset, he jumped up and ran over to me and started thumping the front of the bass drum which was about 4 or 5 foot off the ground. He couldn't get at me because of the water, but he could reach across the water and thump the bass drum. The bouncers came up and threw him out which was a shame because the Kayes' manager, Len, always bought the guy who's drink it was any drink they desired, but this guy never gave Len a chance to ask him. The bass drum had knuckle marks in the front but the drums were not mine, I had borrowed them.

It was while we were working at the nightclub in Port Talbot that a chap used to come and watch the Kayes' act, he had been a professional Boxer and he owned a nightclub himself. He invited us to his place, where he wined and dined us in his private dining room. The waiter came in with good quality bottles of wine, followed by a great big silver tray piled high with mussels cooked in French wine. Every course was fish, it was fantastic. I seem to remember sitting opposite Richard Burton's nephew, who I think was a friend of our host. Our host then came into the room with his chef, who was carrying a salmon that was caught that morning, which he presented to the Kayes. He also gave them a miner's lamp each.

It was the early hours of the morning by now and our host had some friends who were still drinking in his cabaret room. He asked the Kayes if they would entertain his friends, which of course meant Billy and I would also have to play. How could we all refuse? So, into the cabaret room we went, the resident musicians were still there and we asked them if we could borrow their gear for half an hour to save getting ours out of the van. They refused to let us borrow their gear, so we had to unload ours. When our host found out his musicians turned us down, he went mad and gave them a right telling off, but it was their prerogative. We performed for about 45 minutes, then we packed the gear and headed back to our digs. On our way back we were driving through Port Talbot and all the workers were waiting for buses to go to work and we were just getting back from the night before, we had to get some sleep ready for the next night's performance.

Chapter 13

TRAVEL, TRAVEL AND MORE TRAVEL

I loved the drumming and everything it had to offer but the biggest drawback was the travelling and sleeping in my car because I couldn't take a kit of drums into digs when I was on the road. It's always a worry leaving your gear unattended overnight. You are also away from your family a lot. I would go up to the north of England doing one nighters, I would leave home and my son was riding a bike with stabilisers on, when I got back home he's wearing a crash helmet and riding a motor bike. What I'm trying to say is that to some degree you do miss out on watching your child grow up. Speaking of motor bikes, I did buy Eileen a motor bike so she could take Paul to school and also get out and about while I was away, as our cottages were a bit off the beaten track. Eileen's motor bike was a Yamaha 185cc twin cylinder and she looked the part dressed in her crash helmet and leathers. She only needed a whip.

Having finished yet another four-week run with the Kaye Sisters, we were back with Ruby Murray for a week, followed by two weeks with The Morton Fraser Harmonica Gang. Then back to South Wales with a vocalist called Valentino, who I might add was a bit of a heart throb where the ladies were concerned. We finished the Valentino show on the 18th of December and the next day we were in rehearsals at Porthcawl Theatre for Stan Stennett's pantomime, *Cinderella*. Garry Allan played Baron Hard Up and the Ugly Sisters were played by the man and wife team of Howell Evans and his wife Patricia Kane. Howell was a welsh actor, who you would have seen many times on TV as he appeared in *Coronation Street*, *Casualty* and *Open All Hours*, Patricia also appeared in *Open All Hours*, *Little Britain* and *Doctors*. Together they did a great job at being the Ugly Sisters. Cinderella was played by Karon Webb and Prince Charming was played by that lady of song Lesley King. Others in the panto were

Marie Claire, The Falcons, The Winter Mixture and Johnny Stewart as Buttons. Johnny was on BBC 1 with Joe Brown in a show called *Joe and Co.* and had even performed at the London Palladium. Although Stan Stennett had produced the pantomime, he was not in it he was appearing in panto at the Wolverhampton Grand Theatre.

Our pantomime was a great success, it was the first pantomime I had ever done and I enjoyed it, with having to provide drum rolls and sound effects for the knockabout comedy within the panto. We finished in the February and the Wolverhampton one was still running so Stan got Billy and I free tickets to see their panto. We went along and we had good seats at the front, it was great with a few well-known people in it. After the show we went backstage to see Stan and he told us they were having a party and we were invited. When the audience had gone, the stage curtains were closed and some of the band out of the orchestra pit came up on stage to play. Then a load of food appeared as the band started playing and the party was on. One of the stars in the show was Nanette Newman, among other things that she had done in her career was the Fairy Liquid advert on TV, she also appeared in a number of films, in fact she was a talented actress. I asked her for a dance and we chatted, she asked me what I did and I told her I worked on Stan's Summer Shows and Pantos. She was a really nice lady and very attractive, she married Brian Forbes CBE who was an actor and film director. If I remember correctly Lynsey de Paul was also there, she was the first female singer to have a self-written song get to number one in the hit parade. She was another very pretty girl.

Another party we were invited to was at the La Dolce Vita in Birmingham. I remember they had some Limbo Dancers limboing under a bar which they kept lowering and they invited anyone in the room to have a go. Les Dawson was at the party and he got up to try his luck. It was obvious that Les, bless him, had had a few drinks so coupled with that and his pot belly, there was no chance of Les getting under that bar. There he was on his back, stuck, it was so funny and he was a good sport.

Having completed our panto, Billy Pearce and I were in Chelmsford, then London, then Fareham playing for Edmund Hockridge. Edmund did have his own keyboard player and musical director, Jack Martin, who I would play drums with during Edmund's act, he was a great guy. I liked Jack and we enjoyed many glasses of Guinness together. This was during the miners strikes in the 70s which sometimes would cause the venues we were working at to close down for the night due to power cuts. If they closed for the night, we didn't work so we didn't get paid.

We played the 106 club in Fareham and the following night we were back home at a club in Coleshill. The first half of the show went according to plan but come the second half we had a power cut. Edmund Hockridge was due to play the whole of the second half and rather than disappoint the audience, Edmund said he would go on and do his best. The committee somehow managed to get hold of torches and candles, they gave the torches to the people in the front row and put the candles on the stage. We had no microphones and no electric keyboards but they did have an upright piano. Jack Martin knew Edmund's music back to front, so he could play without the music, which we couldn't see anyway, and I played with wire brushes. Edmund had a rich baritone voice, which once again, was a big help. He performed for about an hour and at the end of his act the audience went wild, they stood up clapped and cheered. Technically it was not the best show we ever did, but the reason the audience went wild was because in spite of the problems, we still did the show. A lot of top of the bills would have refused to perform.

Edmund was a Canadian, born in Vancouver, and he had hits with *Hey There, Some Enchanted Evening* and *Young and Foolish*. The last time I saw Edmund was at BBC Pebble Mill, we had gone to see some Rushes of a documentary we had made about Stars in Your Eyes (more of which I will tell you about later). The Rushes are the recording of a show before it is edited, in the break we went for a drink in the bar and Edmund was in there, he told me he was there making a recording for the BBC. Edmund was another nice guy.

During the miners' strike we were on The Searchers show, this time around in the Midlands. We were working in Tamworth, so I took Eileen with me for a change. It was one of those nights when we had a power cut, but this club was prepared for it, they had hired a generator so the show went ahead and we got paid. Frank Allen was the bass player in The Searchers, he gave me his phone number and said anytime we were working in Middlesex we could stay at his place rather than in digs.

After The Searchers we had two weeks with The Dallas Boys. One night we travelled up to the Piccadilly Plaza in Manchester, The

Edmund Hockridge.

Dallas Boys had booked four members from the BBC Northern Dance Orchestra to play with Billy and I, so now we were a six-piece band with these top class musicians. We had to pull out all the stops, which we did and we had a great night. Once again, I packed my drums and drove back to Sutton Coldfield. The following week we were at Trentham Gardens, once again with The Dallas Boys. We did the first half of the show and Syd Lawrence and his Orchestra were booked to do the second half. I was talking to Syd's drummer Fergie Maynard, who played for Syd back in the 70s, he was a good drummer and like all drummers when they meet up, they talk about drums. He did tell me that he liked the sound of my drums which I took as a compliment.

We were back in London, then Fareham and Gosport. This time we were playing for Tony Mercer from *The Black and White Minstrels Show*. We were working in the Petty Officer's mess at HMS Dolphin which was a Royal Navy Submarine School. After the show we were having a drop of Navy Rum and I was talking to one the Petty Officers, we were talking about Submarines and he said if I came back next morning, he would show me around a wartime submarine. So, I met him next morning and he took me on this submarine, I don't know what the name of it was, but it was floating on the water. We had to climb down the conning tower and he let me look through the periscope and I could see across the water towards Davenport, where the HMS Eagle was being dismantled. If you were a tall person of over 6 foot, you were in danger of banging your head. There was a mass of pipes and gauges and engines, the toilets were under the torpedo tubes. How these guys lived in these things I just don't know, to me it was very claustrophobic, I expect modern submarines are a lot better, having said that, it was quite an experience.

The next four weeks saw Billy and I working with Bobby Bennett who presented TVs *Junior Showtime*, Edmund Hockridge, Ruby Murray, Don Maclean (the Birmingham comedian), David Whitfield and Anne Shelton. We were on the Anne Shelton Show and when I was setting up my drums, in came Anne Shelton with her husband, she said, 'Hello everyone,' she was very friendly. She then went into the dressing room where Linda, of Linda and Martin Barry Duo who were also on the show, was fixing her make up. Anne Shelton asked Linda if this was the dressing room that she would be using and Linda, who was a really nice inoffensive girl replied, 'Yes, us two girls are in this dressing room and the guys are in the other dressing room.' Anne then said, 'Do you mean I've got to share a dressing room? I don't share a dressing room with anyone, Darling.'

Well, poor Linda was a bit put out by her attitude, so she went to find her husband Martin, who was putting up their sound system. Linda told him what had happened, then collected her dresses and things and moved into our dressing room to get changed with us. I was still assembling my drums when Anne came on stage and went over to Martin, who was not only performing on the show but was also providing the sound system for everyone as well. She asked him if this was the microphone she was going to use. Now, I have known Martin for many years and he won't take crap from anybody. His answer to Anne was, 'No, this is our microphone and we don't share a microphone with anyone, Darling.' At that, Anne left the stage. I could hear all this and I thought to myself, heck trouble already and we've not even set up yet. A few minutes later Anne's husband came and apologised for the misunderstanding.

Anne Shelton was easy to play for, her songs were *Lili Marleen, Lay Down Your Arms, Surrender to Mine, I'll Never Smile Again* and many more. Ann was given an OBE for a lifetimes work. The night in question did go well in the end and everyone was happy.

It was now time to hitch up the caravan and head off for the summer season. This time we were at the Prince of Wales Theatre in Colwyn Bay. On this show we had top of the bill, our producer Stan Stennett, Roy Lester, The Falcons, Linda and Martin Barry, Bill Gore, Paula Lee Dancing Girls and The Stan Stennett Dancers. We all knew each other and were all friends, which was great. As usual we were invited to a Civic Reception to welcome us to the town, so were invited to the Monks Kitchen in Llandudno. Llandudno was next door to Colwyn Bay, about five miles away and the two places came under the same Entertainments Management. Once again, we were wined and dined but this time I left the white spirits back in Southport.

The following Sunday a certain newspaper wrongly accused us of being involved in sex frolics, which was untrue, all we did was go to the Monks Kitchen for drinks and food, that was it. The following Sunday more was written about us, which once again was untrue, it goes without saying the newspaper had jumped to the wrong conclusions. However, the publicity filled the theatre every night, they were coming to see these sex mechanics and they were asking for our autographs.

We did two different shows a week, number one show and number two show. One night when we got to the interval and as I came out of our compound someone said, 'Hi Mike' and two rows back sat Joe and Betty Robinson from our village Canwell. They had seen our photographs in front of the theatre and came in to see us. Joe had worked with my dad, which I mentioned earlier, it was nice to see them.

Stan Stennett had a lot of friends who would drop in to see the show. A regular visitor was Trevor Ford who played football for Aston Villa, he was also a

Welsh international. One of our dancers was Philippa Boulter, the daughter of John Boulter from *The Black and White Minstrels Show*. We also had Dai Francis, another from *The Black and White Minstrel Show*, come to see us. One night during the interval Stan called Billy and I into his dressing room to meet a friend of his, Denny Wright, who was a jazz guitarist. Denny had played for Humphrey Lyttelton, Lonnie Donegan, Ella Fitzgerald and Stephane Grappelli. Stan gave him his guitar and asked him to play something for us, Denny was amazing, his fingers were a blur.

Our mates who were on the show, Linda and Martin Barry, had a flat just yards away from the stage door. A couple of nights a week they would invite everybody in the show to a party at their flat where they had a bar, a bit like a pub. Come to think of it, my life seems to have been one big party.

Once again it was time to quickly hitch up the caravan and head for home because the following night we were working with Francis Van Dyke who was a violinist. Then we were booked to play for Ronnie Hillton who had hits with *A Windmill in Old Amsterdam* and *The Wonder of You*. Ronnie was another nice guy. For once we were working around the Midlands for a change.

Then we were working yet again with Edmund Hockridge, Bob Monkhouse, the Kaye Sisters and The Dallas Boys. Another act I would like to mention that I played for a few times was The Minitones who were two midgets, Kenny Baker and Jack Purvis, they were a really good act. Kenny was born in Birmingham and both he and Jack had appeared in films. You may remember Kenny, he played R2-D2 in *Star Wars*, Jack was also in *Star Wars*. Kenny was just under four foot tall, sadly he's no longer with us, he was a lovely chap.

We had to dash down to Chelmsford on the Barron Nights Show at Marconi's Social Club, a really nice club that we worked at a number of times. This brought us up to another four weeks in Stars in Your Eyes, still around the Midlands, so I was able to get home each night. Then once again it was panto time, I hitched up the caravan and took it to Porthcawl to do Stan Stennett's *Mother Goose*. The line-up was Stan, Wally Dunn, Marie Claire, Ella Lightfoot, Bryn Williams, Christine Treeby, Sian Hopkins, The Winter Mixture, Stan's People Dance Troupe and Peter Lewis. I was in the caravan on my own for the first week because Paul was now at school. We did a week's rehearsal and during the rehearsals the Welsh TV came round to the theatre and filmed everyone in the panto in their costumes. Stan said to Billy and I, go and play something and the TV crew will film you. So, we played a swing number, they had this big camera complete with a very strong light and they filmed Billy playing, then swung across to film me. I looked at the camera and smiled when suddenly I dropped a drum stick, now this stick bounced on the cymbal and I quickly caught it and carried on playing, still smiling. When it came on the TV News that night, my dropping of the stick looked like a trick, when really it was a cock up. There must have been loads of welsh drummers trying to master this trick.

On Christmas Eve, I dashed back home to spend Christmas Day with the family. On Boxing Day morning I took Eileen and Paul with me back to Porthcawl, I dropped them off at the caravan then I had to dash off to the theatre to do the opening matinee performance. After the show I went back to the caravan to see if Eileen was okay and have something to eat and then back to the theatre to do the night show. When I got back Eileen was all upset and Paul was in bed with a bandage around his head. When I asked what had happened, Eileen said an Alsatian dog had torn his ear off. Eileen had to go to the woman in the opposite caravan to ask if she would take her and Paul to the hospital, which the lady very kindly had done. They went to Bridgend Hospital where his ear was sewn back on, his fingers were also bandaged where the dog had bitten them, he was only five years old at this time.

All this had happened within a few hours of us arriving there. When Paul woke up I said, 'You okay, son? Do you want a drink?' He said, 'No dad. I've only got one ear.' I was very worried about him and not only that I had to go back and do the night performance and with it being the opening day and night of the panto, there are a certain amount of nerves, so I was a bit uptight to say the least. After the show I dashed back to Eileen and Paul, there were no mobile phones in those days, so I couldn't phone to see how Paul was. However, Paul was a tough little lad and the next day a woman came by to ask how Paul was, she had heard what had happened. This lady had a little dog with her and Paul immediately made a fuss of her little dog, so the ordeal didn't put him off dogs. Eventually the Alsatian was put down and Paul recovered, but if you think about it, the outcome could have been a lot worse.

On a lighter note, Billy Pearce and Peter Lewis shared a big static caravan on Trecco Bay for the season and they used to travel together to the theatre every day. One night Peter asked me if I could drop him off at their caravan because Billy was staying in Porthcawl for the night and they were in Billy's car so Peter was stuck for a lift. I gave him a lift and when we got to his caravan Peter discovered he had left his keys in the dressing room back at the theatre so couldn't open the caravan door. I had a look at the window and realised if I had a carving knife, I could push it through the rubber seal, flick the window catch and open the window. So, Peter went off to get a knife, ten minutes later he was back with a carving knife, where he had got it from at that time in the morning, I've no idea.

The knife did the trick and I got the window open, Peter crawled through the window and as he pulled his legs through I heard a crash and a load of very colourful bad language. He had put his foot into a bucket that he and Billy had been peeing in for days and the contents of the bucket had spilt all over the caravan floor. Peter opened the door, 'Come in, Mike would you like a cup of coffee?' Well, to be honest with the smell of Calor gas mixed with the smell of the pee, I politely turned down the offer of a coffee and told him I would see him tomorrow.

On the last night of the panto season we would play jokes on each other. Stan Stennett didn't like us to play these last night jokes, unless we told him what we intended to do, then he would say yes or no. Wally Dunn who was Mother Goose would come on stage and say to Billy, 'Mr Piano Man can you give me a Chord,' then Billy would throw a length of washing-line up to Mother Goose. Then Mother Goose would say to me, 'Mr Drummer can you give me a roll please,' then I would throw a bread roll up to him. It was all very corny but the kids in the audience would laugh their socks off at it. We did this every night for nine weeks, then I came up with idea of getting a small loaf, cutting a hole in the bottom and filling it with talcum powder. I told Stan and he thought it would be okay. Mother Goose came on stage and went through the routine, 'Mr Drummer can you give me a roll please,' so I threw the loaf. If I had done it a dozen times, I could not have done it better. The talcum powder went all over his head and face, he looked like a ghost. Mother Goose was completely taken by surprise and the look on his face had the audience in stitches with laughter, but that was not the end of it. The talcum powder had gone all over the stage and made it very slippery, so when the dancers came on stage they were going arse over tip slipping on the talcum powder, it was so funny.

I had already taken Eileen and Paul back home some weeks before because of Paul going back to school and I had to stay and finish the remaining few weeks of the panto season. After the last night I packed my gear, said goodbye to the cast, picked the caravan up and travelled through the night back home, ready to play the following night in Coventry with the Wedgewoods. After the Wedgewoods it was the Bryn Phillips Show (from *The Comedians*), followed by the Malcolm Vaughan Show. Malcolm had his own keyboard player, his Musical Director whose name was Garry, I can't remember his surname but he was a good player. I enjoyed playing for Malcolm he had a few hits *St Therese of The Roses, More Than Ever, My Special Angel* and many more, Malcolm was a nice guy. Garry stayed with us at our cottage for the week we worked together. Garry wrote some music for The Grumbleweeds, I think it was their signature tune, but I can't be sure of that. Whatever he wrote in our kitchen, I delivered it to The Grumbleweeds at the Alexandra Theatre in Birmingham.

By now Stars in Your Eyes had matured into a first-class show and was becoming very popular around clubland. So now we were on a ten-week tour of South Wales, North Wales, Southampton, London and the Midlands. One of the venues we played was Long Lartin Prison. I arrived early and went through the big main doors into the prison. The prison officers on the gate sent me to another officer who had an Alsatian dog and was standing by a 25 foot high fence with a gate in it. I drove through the gate and the officer with the dog said, 'You see that green door, pull up there and someone will help you unload.' So I did what I was told, I got out of my car when the green door opened and this chap came out and unloaded my gear, I didn't carry anything. This chap asked me if that was the lot, I said yes and I thanked him, he said, 'that's okay' and then disappeared. The officer said, 'Do you know who that was?' I said, 'I've no idea.' He said, 'That was Roy James he drove the getaway car for the Great Train Robbers.' He was serving 30 years for his part in the robbery, he was a racing driver and he had won trophies, after he had served 11 years he was let out of prison. However, he ended up in prison again for shooting his father-in-law, who fortunately survived, but Roy got another six years imprisonment.

We played in a sort of gymnasium, it had a large stage and lighting but we carried our own lighting and scenery, our roadie was also our lighting engineer. Everybody arrived and we got set up ready to start, the prisoners were ushered in and sat down. Billy Pearce and I played in front of the stage, so we were only about seven feet away from the prisoners in the front row. When we got the show started and our dancers came on showing their legs like dancers do, the prisoners' eyes were popping out, they probably hadn't seen legs like that in years. When the interval came, they had urns of tea, coffee and sandwiches for us. No alcohol. We had programmes with our photographs and a write up about each one of us in the show, we normally sold these programmes but on this occasion we gave each prisoner a free programme. Some of the prisoners wanted our autographs, so they would send one of the warders up to us with their programme to be signed. I found it very difficult to look into the audience and smile, knowing that there were some real hard cases amongst them to say the least.

The Bristol Locarno was another great place to work, Billy and I were on the revolving stage and the show worked on the dance floor. Stars in Your Eyes was a three hour show, but when we worked the Locarno we only had to do half an hour while the big band had a break. So, what we would do was a *Jesus Christ Superstar* or a Rock and Roll scene or whatever we had in the show at that time.

At the end of the ten-week tour, we were with Larry Grayson at the Wolverhampton Theatre for a one nighter. We had Barry Young and Les Girls, Steve Ford, The Lyntones, Bill Gore, Del Derrick, Billy Pearce and I, plus the bass player off TV's *Lunch Box*, Ken Ingerfield and Larry Grayson's Musical Director, Dennis Ploughwright. We did the rehearsals then went for a drink, we ended up getting Dennis tipsy, somebody nicknamed him Dolly. He was worried in case Larry found out he had been drinking (when Larry appeared on TV you would always see Dennis playing for him). The theatre was packed and the show was great, our band played well and Larry was brilliant.

Paul attended the same school that I had when I was his age. Each year they held a sports day and when it got to the fathers' race, Paul said, 'Go on Dad, have a go.' So I was lined up with the local farmers and bang we were off, it was an obstacle course, getting under a tarpaulin etc, would you believe I won it two years running. It must have been all that running away from those girlfriend's fathers all those years ago that kept me fit and, of course, Paul was delighted that I had won.

We did more work with David Whitfield, then it was time to go into summer season yet again and we were back at the Prince of Wales Theatre, Colwyn Bay. I took the caravan and I was on my own because Paul hadn't yet broke up from school for the summer holidays. It was a different show from the year before, this time we had, of course, Stan Stennett with Lesley King, Peter Lewis, Linda and Martin Barry, Johnny Stewart, The Maljohns, a dance troupe and Billy and I. The Maljohns were the only act we did not know, they came to us from the London Palladium and were a great acrobatic act. They impressed everyone with their twisting, turning and somersaulting and if that was not enough they made you laugh as well.

This time we were performing three different shows a week, so anyone on holiday for a week could see three shows. We did a lot of rehearsing during the day to keep on top of performing three different shows a week. As usual I had to dash back home to collect Eileen and Paul and bring them back to Colwyn Bay for six weeks, then I would have to take them back home for Paul to go back to school. Then once again I would return to finish the season.

In the foyer of the Theatre, by the box office, were two prizes that could be won, one prize was a fridge and the other prize was a Chopper bike which was the bike to have in those days. In the one show, Johnny Stewart would come on stage and pretend to insult Billy and in turn Billy would say, 'If you're going to speak to me like that I'm off.' At that, Billy would climb over the rail of our compound and walk away, leaving the audience thinking it was for real. Then Johnny would turn to me and I would say, 'You have upset my mate, so I'm off as well.' Then I would walk up the incline of the theatre to the box office. Johnny would do ten minutes of comedy, then we would wander back as though nothing had happened.

I had the idea of borrowing the Chopper bike, so one afternoon I went and got it and wheeled it down to my drums and covered it up with my drum sheet. I also borrowed a raincoat and a cap. Later that night in the show Johnny came on stage and did the routine, when he got to me I said, 'You have upset my mate, so I'm off as well.' Then I put on the raincoat and cap, uncovered the Chopper and pushed it up the incline and into the foyer as though I was going home, then put the Chopper back in its place. Meanwhile Johnny was in fits of laughter and so were the audience, in fact the routine went really well. When the interval came Stan sent for me in his dressing room, he gave me a rollocking because they had the North Wales Police driving round scouring the streets looking for the Chopper, Stan thought it had been stolen, he had to phone the Police to call off the search and explain what had happened.

One of the visitors to the show was Nigel Davenport who was better known for being in films such as *Chariots of Fire* and TV's *Howard's Way*, his daughter Amanda was one of our dancers and Nigel used to come and see Amanda and see the show. But the most famous celebrity we had come to see us was Stan's mate Eric Morecambe of Morecambe and Wise. Eric came round to our dressing room and introduced himself, I asked him for his autograph and I had a glass jar of peanut brittle so Eric signed the label, not before having a couple of pieces for himself. Eric was good fun and he chatted to us until it was time to start the show.

Stan had told us that Eric was paying us a visit so I got Eileen and Paul tickets for the night, Stan had also put it about the town that Eric would be there so the theatre was packed out. Stan had reserved a seat for Eric and he asked us to show Eric to his seat. The dressing rooms were under the stage, so the three of us climbed the stairs from below and we opened the door into the Auditorium and we were met with an outburst of applause and cheering, it was amazing. It sent a tingle down the back of my neck. Eric was smoking a big cigar and above the door was an illuminated sign saying No Smoking. We took him to his seat, then went into our compound and started the show. When the interval came, Stan invited Eric onto the stage and as he came up he came over to me, leaned over into our compound and lifted one of my cymbals and said, 'Mike Not Stew Again,' and the audience just fell about laughing. Stan and Eric had a bit of fun together for a few minutes much to the audience's delight. After the show the newspaper reporters took some photographs, then Eric came round to say goodbye and I introduced him to Eileen and Paul. He then shook hands with everybody and said goodbye. What a night that was.

Above: A gig with Denise Lewis OBE (left). On the drums (right).
Below: Jimmy Cricket with me, Michael and my mom.

Above: Stars In Your Eyes. I'm in the red shirt on the right.
Below: Bill Gore's Oompah Band.

The older I get the more I look like my dad.

*Back: Mike Sullivan, Andy Brown,
Paul Woodall. Front: Steve Morgan,
Keith Sealy and me.*

Garry Allcock and myself.

John Evans and me.

Alpha One swing band.

Tilly Critchley, Noddy Holder and myself.

The Roly Polys

Above: The Roly Polys' promotional photograph taken by myself.
Below: Prince of Wales Theatre me with dancing girls and John Baugh.

Me with TV weather girl Charlie Neil.

Me, Dave Evans (Lee Evans' father) and Mark Bettis.

John Roberts, Mike Sullivan and me.

Eileen and myself.

Eileen's great cooking.

With Noel Edmonds at Drayton Manor.   *Francisco with the harp.*

*Back row from left to right: Peter Lewis, J.P. James, Ollie Spencer, myself,
Bill Gore, Martin Barry, Pat Ramsey from The Roly Polys, Bob Ingham, Mike Carter.
Front row: dancing girls.*

Above: Paul, Keri and our grandchildren.
Below: Myself and Eileen the day we sold the shop.

Yet another enjoyable summer season came to an end and as usual I had taken Eileen and Paul back home so Paul could go back to school and once again I would go back and finish the season. The gear was packed and the caravan hooked up and I drove through the night. The next week we were back in Stars in Your Eyes for four weeks, once again we were travelling around from town to town.

There are some other acts I've worked with who deserve a mention. There was Iris Williams OBE, Iris had worked with Rosemary Clooney and Bob Hope, she had also appeared on a Royal Variety Show. Iris had worked on some high-class shows in her time and she also had a song in the hit parade called *He Was Beautiful*. She was a great jazz singer as well. I worked down the South of England with Iris ending up at the Margate Winter Gardens. The show was Bert Weedon, Colin Crompton (from the *Wheel Tappers and Shunters* TV Show) and of course Iris Williams. Mike and Bernie Winters did the week before us at the Winter Gardens, I got talking to Mike Winters and I asked him what sort of week had they had? He said they had a good week and with our line-up so should we.

When we were at Margate, I was a bit hard up with no money, so I was sleeping in my car. What I did to get something to eat, I chatted up the girls in the sandwich bar and they gave me a few sandwiches in a bag and they gave me free cups of tea. God bless those girls they kept me going for most of the week. After each show I would leave my dinner suit on and stand at the bar, then someone would recognise the fact I was part of the show and would offer to buy me a drink. Billy Pearce was staying in a bed and breakfast place and his room was on the ground floor with two beds. So, a couple of times Billy smuggled me through the window and I did get a few nights sleep in a bed. When you are on the road and hard up you find a way to survive. Now, you may be thinking why didn't I borrow some money off someone? Well, I could have done that but at the end of the day you have still got to pay it back, then you're back to square one again. Anyway, at the end of the week I got paid and things were back to normal.

One day Billy and I walked down to the Lido Theatre where Carl Wayne was working in a summer show as was Charlie Drake, they said, 'Hi lads, how you doing?' We told them we were working up the road and they told us they were having trouble with their band, did we want the job? We had to say no because we were already committed.

Iris Williams married a friend of mine, Clive Pyatt, otherwise known as Clive Brandy due to the fact he drank brandy and coke. Clive was a real character, he could sell sand to the Arabs. Clive and Iris owned a pub called The Pheasant Plucker in Berkshire, try saying that when you have had a drink. We were working on a show where Clive was compere and on the show was a Paraguayan Harp player called Francisco Yglesia, who was a former member of Los Paraguayos. Francisco was a brilliant act, one of the best acts I have played for and when he had finished his act the audience would go wild because they had never seen an act like his before. He was dressed in traditional Paraguayan costume and played tunes on his harp, tunes like *La Bamba, Bell Bird, Cascada, Love Story* and many more, all brilliantly played. At the time he didn't speak much English. Each night at the end of his act the audience would be cheering, Clive would bring him back on stage and ask him what he thought of the English audience, Francisco didn't really know what to say.

One night Francisco asked me in his broken English what could he say in reply? I told him to say 'Piss Off.' So off he went practising in his broken English, 'Pizzz off, Pizzz off, Pizzz off.' Later that night when Clive called him back on stage and said, 'Francisco, what do you think of the English audiences?' Francisco replied with a big smile, 'Pizzz off.' Well, the audience fell about laughing and Clive stood there with his mouth open, then he responded with, 'Get your donkey out of the dressing room and you piss off.' Of course Francisco thought he was being polite, he smiled and left the stage. I taught him some more swear words and it was so funny to hear him swear in his broken English. The one day he went into Boots the chemist for something, the girl behind the counter gave him what he had asked for, then Francisco smiled and said 'Pizzz off,' and calmly walked away, leaving the poor girl wondering what she had done wrong. Francisco now lives in England and speaks and understands English much better these days. Francisco tours the world on ships etc, entertaining and he tells the story of the drummer who taught him to swear.

Another very funny guy was Billy Dainty. Billy was in fact a local chap, he came from Dudley. Billy used to do a funny walk in his act and the drummer had to play a military rhythm to fit his funny walk, this was where my military training came in handy. Billy was another nice guy. As was Ross McManus, who is Ross McManus I hear you say? Ross used to sing and play trumpet for Joe Loss. Ross and Rose Brennan both sang together for Joe Loss. I worked with Ross a few times and I remember Ross putting his sound system up one night and he said, 'This is a new system, my son has bought it for me.' His son was Elvis Costello the pop singer and Elvis was married to Diana Krall the Canadian jazz pianist and vocalist.

Having finished another four weeks of Stars in Your Eyes, we were back with Gerry Monroe, then Malcolm Vaughan for a couple of weeks, plus a few shows with Bert Weedon, Bryn Phillips and Hope and Keen who were cousins. Their fathers were comedians Syd and Max Harrison. We were now back in pantomime at the Palace Theatre in Redditch. It was once again *Cinderella*. After panto it was back down the south with The Dallas Boys, then a week with Danny Williams, then back home with our girl next door Ruby Murray.

Our agent Bernard Parr was asked by ATV Television if he could send someone to their Studios in Birmingham to work on their soap opera *Crossroads*, so Bernard sent me. I had to take a photograph and I got the job. It was mostly extra and walk-on parts, although they did give me a speaking part which I got paid more money for, I was told what I had to say. So, there I was behind the camera repeating my lines over and over again, waiting for the floor manager to give me my cue to walk on and deliver my lines. It's quite nerve-racking knowing you have to get it right.

One scene I was in, was when Noele Gordon got engaged to John Bentley, in other words Meg Richardson and Hugh Mortimer. I was in the engagement party scene and I played the part of a friend of Vera Downend, the Hairdresser played by Zeph Gladstone. This scene had to be rehearsed several times because there were quite a few people in the scene and we were bumping into each other. There was a buffet and bottles of wine, and each time we ran through the scene we were eating chicken legs and Hugh Mortimer was opening bottles of wine and filling our glasses. Well, this happened several times and drinking in the morning before lunchtime meant some of us were getting a bit worse for wear. Zeph Gladstone and I were sitting on a sofa when Zeph said to me, 'I've dropped an earring.' The next minute she was on her knees under the sofa looking for her earring, with her bum sticking up in the air. And may I say with the greatest respect, what a nice bum it was. When she came up for air, she looked at me and said, 'Do you know I'm pissed.' However, we did get the scene right in the end. I liked Zeph, she was a lovely lady.

Another scene I was in was when they had a Casino/Night Club. I seem to remember having to go down some steps to it. There was me and another chap in this scene and our job was to pretend we were leaving the club. After we had left, there was the sound of a car pulling up outside the club, then the sound of footsteps followed by the sound of breaking glass and then a Molotov Cocktail Bomb came through the window and set the place on fire. Well, that was the plan, but the trouble was when they tried to get the bomb to go through the toffee glass window, it kept bouncing back outside (toffee glass is a pretend glass, very brittle and easy broken, like you see on the films when someone gets hit over the head with a bottle). We had to wait while they changed the toffee glass each time. When they did get it right and the bomb came through the window, the crew had got a Calor gas bottle connected to a tube with holes in it underneath the camera lens, which was already alight on a very low flame. As the bomb came through the window, they turned up the flame in front of the camera which made it look like the place was on fire.

I was in ten episodes of *Crossroads* all together (I could have had a regular job in *Crossroads* but I kept remembering my lines). Just a joke. John Forgeham was also in *Crossroads* at that time, he lived in Sutton Coldfield by Sutton Park and I used to give him a lift home. He also did a comedy act, he used to ask me to ask Bernard Parr to give him some work. The trouble was I had been told he used bad language and I knew Bernard wouldn't stand for that, so I made excuses as to why I hadn't told Bernard about him. John was married to Fiesta Mei Ling who was an actress, you would have seen in many films.

We were all set for a twelve-week tour of Stars in Your Eyes and once again we were on our travels London, Fareham, Southampton, Portsmouth, Plymouth and Cornwall. For the first time we were playing the North East of England, Newcastle, Middlesbrough, Gateshead, Durham, Stockton, Sunderland, Hartlepool, Redcar, Saltburn and many other places.

It was while we were working in Portsmouth one of the acts, Paul Fox who was a Juggler in the show, broke his arm and had to leave the show. Not only did he perform his act in the show, he was also in one of the comedy sketches. So I was asked if I would take his place, which I did. The sketch involved having two ventriloquist's dummies, Karl Rainer had one and I had the other. I would say, 'Ladies and Gentlemen my friend Karl Rainer will now recite the alphabet whilst drinking a glass of water.' Then Karl would drink the water and work the dummy's mouth at the same time, while I would be saying the alphabet through the microphone, but the audience would be watching Karl. Then, in turn, Karl would say, 'Ladies and Gentlemen our drummer Mike Rubery will drink a glass of water whilst counting up to ten.' Then I would drink the water and work the dummy's mouth and Karl would be counting, but the audience would be watching me. We had been doing this for a couple of weeks but instead of water I drank Guinness, I used to put the glass of Guinness in the footlights before the start of the show. When it was time for the sketch, I would get off the drums and get up on stage.

On this particular night I was doing my bit on stage when I noticed all the cast standing in the wings watching, I thought it was strange, but I had to concentrate on what I was doing. When it was time for Karl to say, 'Our drummer Mike Rubery will drink a glass of water whilst counting up to ten,' I picked up my glass and drank my drink. And wallop! I couldn't get my breath. What they had done was empty out most of the Guinness and replaced it with Woods Old Navy Rum, 100%. I was gasping for breath, even the dummy's eyes were watering and, of course, everyone was standing in the wings in fits of laughter, all good fun.

On another occasion we were working at the MG Car Works in Cowley and as usual Billy and I were set up in front of the stage. We finished the first half with a Western scene, Karl Rainer who was the principal male vocalist in the show, came on stage dressed as a cowboy singing *Oh What A Beautiful Morning*. Following Karl's song there was a drum solo leading into a Red Indian dance performed by our dancers. Halfway through Karl's song my drum stool broke in two pieces and I ended up flat on my back, the top of my seat rolled into the audience, it must have looked so funny. The audience were laughing, so was Karl, Billy and the dancers. Karl couldn't get his words out for laughing and I was running around trying to find something to sit on to play this drum solo for the Red Indian dance. I ended up sitting on a chair that was too low. I must have looked a right clown but I did what I had to do, I was glad when the interval came so I could find something better to sit on. A chap from the audience gave me back the top of my drum stool but it was no good I had to buy a new one.

The twelve-week tour came to an end and we were doing odd shows with people like Yana whose biggest hit was *Climb up the Wall*. Yana was a good-looking lady and sexy with it, apparently she was a lesbian, although she had been married and I heard that she also had a fling with George Formby, but I must say she was a nice looking lady.

We were working on a show at the Carlton Suite in Liskeard, Cornwall when we had a phone call from our agent Bernard Parr in Birmingham telling us not to go back home, but to go to the Isle of Wight as quick as we could. We had to go to the The Showboat Theatre on Shanklin Pier. What had happened was, they had sacked their band because they couldn't play for cabaret, they couldn't read music and were more of a rock band, the wrong band for the job. When we got there, they had fixed us up with bed and breakfast, I was in one place and Billy was in another place. I was with a young couple and it was a very nice place.

On the afternoon of our first night we were rehearsing the acts and were told that there was a guitarist booked to play with us as well. As we were rehearsing the door opened and in walked this weedy looking chap wearing glasses that looked like the bottoms of beer glasses. He had a guitar case in one hand and an amplifier in the other hand, struggling to walk up the room. I said to Billy, 'If he's a musician I'll eat my hat.' He introduced himself as Steve Levinson, he was a little Jewish chap from Holloway, London. He told us he had just finished working with Millicent Martin.

We had finished our rehearsal and little Steve had set up his gear and we asked him what he wanted to play, he said what about *Shaft* from the film of the same name? Away we went and he turned out to a brilliant player, *Shaft* became our opening number every night. Little Steve turned out to be a smashing chap and a good player, so it looked like I had to put some salt and pepper on my hat.

Each week we had a different act come from the mainland to perform with our resident acts and we would have to rehearse with them once a week. It was just after we had finished rehearsing one of these acts, when someone came knocking on the door and waving. So, I went to see who it was and to my great surprise it was Miss X, she was with her husband and some friends. They had seen our photographs at the entrance of the pier. She was paying me a lot of attention, which made me a feel a bit awkward, with her husband being there. I took them to the pub at the back of the theatre called The Crow's Nest, we all had a drink and she was chatting to me, not bothering with her husband and friends. I could see in her eyes that the spark was still there. When I had a chance, I said to Billy give it five minutes and then say, 'Mike we will have to go because of getting back for tonight's Show.' So that's what we did to get out of the situation, I made my apologies, said goodbye and left. It was always a worry for me that Miss Y could be on holiday at one of these places we were working. If I bumped into her, I would have some awkward questions to answer.

Meanwhile back at my bed and breakfast digs, the lady of the house, after her husband had gone to work would bring me breakfast in bed. I've never heard of any bed and breakfast places where the lady of the house brings you breakfast in bed. She would never knock on the door, just walk in with a tray of breakfast. She would kneel-down at the side of the bed and watch me eat my breakfast. This was fine, but she would put her hands in funny places. It was plain to see she had got her eye on me. After I had had my breakfast she always wanted to kiss me. I was getting a bit worried, if ever her husband came back, how would I explain things? So, I went and hired a caravan, with the excuse that my wife and young son were coming to stay with me, which was true. They were due to travel from Birmingham to Southsea and then catch the Hovercraft over to Ryde, where I had arranged to meet them and take them to the caravan. I was able to say goodbye to my amorous landlady, it was a bit like one the *Carry On* Films. Just imagine me running down the road with an angry husband running after me shaking his fist.

Eileen and I loved the Isle of Wight, we explored the whole island. One day we were driving down a country lane when I drove over what I though was a length of rope, it turned out to be a snake. I stopped the car, Paul and I got out to see what it was and found an adder just under three foot long, it was warming itself on the warm tarmac. Eileen wouldn't get out of the car, it was dead, well I had run over it. Osborne House was always worth a visit, it was Queen Victoria's home, a magnificent place. Then there was Cowes where the sailing boats are anchored, we saw the tall ships when they sailed into the Isle of Wight. The roads on the island were not built for speeding, the only road with any length was the military road.

Once again it was time for Eileen and Paul to go back home. Karl Rainer's wife and two daughters, who had been staying with him, also had to return home. Karl and I could not drive our families back home because it was just too far and we would not be able to get back in time. So, we took them on the ferry to the mainland then put them on the train back to Birmingham, then we went back to finish the season. Karl had rented a room in a big house in Bembridge for his family and he suggested that I move in with him now our families had gone back home. We shared the rent which worked out cheaper for both of us. We got friendly with the guy who owned the house, who told us that the original drawings of the Islander Aircraft were drawn up in the house we were staying in. The Islander Aircraft was made by Britten Norman at Bembridge, it was a very successful Aircraft. Our landlord took Karl and I to the factory where they made the Islander. I think our landlord had something to do with the factory, because the people who worked there seemed to know him. It was very interesting to see these planes being built.

There is a lot of hard work involved in show business but there's also a lot of fun. The trouble with the acts of today is they stick a disc into a machine and sing to it, so there's no atmosphere coming from the stage. When you have musicians playing for acts, there's more atmosphere coming from the stage and the audience enjoys it a lot more. The acts of today don't know what they are missing and they certainly haven't had the fun we had, in fact they have not served their apprenticeship in show business. They have never really learned the business. They have never gone through the rough times in order to learn their craft. In fact, modern technology makes it too easy for them.

Our guitarist Steve Levinson, considering he was a musician, was very naïve, on one occasion Steve had to get special permission from his Rabbi in Holloway to play on one of their religious occasions. The Rabbi did give him permission to play. We used to do our fair share of drinking and Steve tried to keep up with us, wanting to be one of the lads. One night he had a few too many and I gave him a lift back to his digs. The next night he came up to me and said, 'Mike the next time I have a drink can you take me back to your digs?' I said, 'Yes. Why what's wrong?' He told me that he had got into bed and during the night he had to get up to go to the toilet and in his drunken stupor instead of going to the toilet he had gone into his landlord's daughter's bedroom and peed all over her while she was in bed asleep. His landlord went berserk at Steve and threatened to throw him out if ever he did anything like that again. So, whenever he had been drinking I would take him back with me and Karl to keep him out of trouble.

The season came to an end and I must say the Isle of Wight is one of my favourite places. We had to get back home quick because we were working in Wolverhampton the following night. Sadly, Shanklin Pier was blown down in a big storm, it broke up the Pier and it was damaged beyond repair.

We were booked to play at the Midland Hotel, as it was called at that time, by New Street Station in Birmingham. It was for the Japanese Airlines staff party and they were drinking Saki out of small wooden boxes. The first prize in the raffle was a round the world trip, courtesy of Japanese Airlines. Now that's what you call a raffle prize.

We were on a show with Jim Davidson and a Dutchman called Vout Steenhuis, who was a brilliant guitarist. We had played for Vout before and he was a nice guy, we used to have jam sessions together before the audience came in. We also had Los del Paraquayos on the bill. One night we were all working at Aberystwyth Football Club, I had taken the caravan with Eileen and Paul and we parked up on the car park. The Welsh legend, Mike England MBE, was there he was a Welsh International footballer, who became the Welsh Team Manager for many years (for a Welshman with a name like England I bet he got his leg pulled). He took us all for a kick about on their ground and after we had finished playing football we had a shower and then went back to the caravan. Eileen made a load of sandwiches and cups of tea, our caravan was full up. I had a TV that I ran off the car battery and it so happened that Jim Davidson, who was sat with us in the caravan, had a TV show that was on at that time. He asked if he could watch the programme, so I switched it on and he watched himself but he didn't seem to be happy with his performance. He stood up and walked out, he left without saying thank you, he just walked out. All the other guys made a fuss of Eileen and thanked her for the sandwiches and tea. I did a lot of work with Jim Davidson and he was a very funny guy, but as a person I didn't really like him.

Before we knew it, we were back in Stars in Your Eyes for another eight weeks. We toured the Midlands, South Wales and the South of England. Having finished the eight weeks we were back at Long Lartin Prison and once again it was for the prisoners. We had Bryn Phillips from *The Comedians* TV show and the compere was our old mate Clive Brandy and when he came out on stage his opening line was, 'Who's been a naughty boy then?' Well, you should have heard the uproar from the prisoners, all in good spirit, I might add. By the way, this time I had to carry my drums myself, there was no sign of Roy James the train robber. The prison had a nice football pitch, but apparently all the football matches they played were home games.

On the 9th of January 1975, Billy and I were asked to play for Bill Gore for the Guinness Book of Records, he was attempting to beat the World Record for

Yodelling. Well, he did beat the record, he yodelled for 5 hours and 3 minutes but at the end I don't know who was the worse for wear me, Billy or Bill Gore, but Bill couldn't work for a couple of weeks afterwards until his throat had recovered. Back in the 1980s I became the drummer in Bill Gore's Bavarian Oompah Band. We did several West Midlands Radio Programmes at Pebble Mill with Malcom Boyden. I used to take a snare drum into the studio and play everything on that. Malcom Boyden asked me to play something on my own, so I just played a few bars ending in a drum roll and this was live on radio, later that drum fill was used as part of the advertisement for Radio West Midlands.

The funny thing was, although Bill would dress in Bavarian style clothes and yodel he had never been to Switzerland, but he had been to see *The Sound Of Music* thirty-three times. He used to say when he was a baby he didn't cry he yodelled. Bill came from Carlisle and was booked to work with Norman Wisdom at the Alexandra Theatre in Birmingham. It was while working in Birmingham he met his future wife Christine, who said it was love at first sight.

We made a record with Bill Gore and one the tracks was *In a Monastery Garden* in which he was to demonstrate his expertise at whistling. As normal for a drummer I was in a booth on my own with microphones over the drums. When the light came on for us to start playing and Bill to start his whistling, he whistled a few bars then he stopped the band and stopped the recording. The engineer's voice came across our headphones asking what was wrong? Bill replied, 'My false teeth have come out.' So, we had to wait while Bill put some super glue on his teeth. The light came on again and away we went, this time his whistling was a success and so was the rest of the recording.

We were now down in The New Forest, then back up to London finishing up at Wandsworth Prison on the Helen Shapiro Show. Helen was not just a pop singer she was also a good jazz singer. She was only 14 years of age when she came to fame, singing hits like *Walking Back to Happiness* and *You Don't Know*. We didn't have to play for her as she had her own trio, The Bill Colman Trio, we played for the other acts on the show.

After Helen Shapiro we were working with The Swinging Blue Jeans, Bert Weedon, Bobby Bennett, then down to London with Los Reales Del Paraguay, stopping to make a quick recording at the Highbury Recording Studio in London. We finished the week, then back home to work with comedian George Roper. We then started a nine-week tour of Stars in Your Eyes, working in places like the Castaways in Birmingham and the Princess Theatre in Clacton. Then back down to the South of England, South Wales and finishing in London. We stayed on in London to work a week with our old mate Bert Weedon, followed by a week in Cornwall, still working with Bert. Then back home to meet up with Billy Fury, this time we didn't get into any punch ups and he was early every night. After Billy Fury we travelled around with acts like Ray Fell and Shep's Banjo Boys. We worked in Dartmoor Prison which had been built for Napoleonic war prisoners, also American War prisoners, in later years it was a prison for criminals of the day such as Mad Frankie Fraser and Jack 'The Hat' McVitie.

We were then at The Severn Manor Hotel in Stourport working with Emile Ford for a week. He was born in the West Indies and was the first black singer to have a hit in the UK with *What Do You Want To Make Those Eyes At Me For?* I didn't find him an easy chap to work with, in fact he was another person I didn't really like. The next time we were on the Emile Ford Show, sometime later, he was singing to C90 tapes. He was the first act that I came across to be self-contained by singing to these tapes but like I said earlier, there was no atmosphere coming from the stage. Seeing him singing to these tapes made me realise something and that was he was not happy with any of the musicians that played for him.

In August 1975 we were down in the South of England and on the show were a Birmingham group called Sight and Sound. Their drummer was a chap called Roger Spencer who lived near to Sutton Coldfield. When two drummers get together they become friends and that's what happened to Roger and I, we are still good pals to this day. Roger performed the comedy in the group's act and not long after we met, Roger left the group and started a new career as a comedian under the new name of Ollie Spencer. Ollie became a much sought-after comedian, so much so that he became the warm-up man for the TV show *Tiswas*. He also did some writing for *Tiswas* as well as performing in it. He did a spell on the *Comedians* TV show. Ollie very often comes round to our house for a cup of tea and a biscuit or a piece of cake, but don't tell his wife Olga, because he's supposed to be slimming. I can honestly say Ollie is a top guy.

Still down south, this time with The Ivy League. Then back home to join a brand-new show called Clubland Follies for five weeks. Having completed Clubland Follies we went into Stars in Your Eyes for another eight weeks. Once again more travelling, another spell in the North East and then back down to the London area. We played Millwall Baths and at the end of the night, when it was time to load up our big van with our road manager, outside was a bunch of yobs with knifes sharpening bits of wood. They were waiting for the chance to steal our gear. We had to pull down the van's shutter each time we put anything in it, plus we had to leave a couple of our guys standing by the van until we were all loaded up. The manager of the baths asked us if we would give him a lift home because he was in danger of being mugged by these yobs. So, I'm in no hurry to go back to Millwall.

We decided not to go away for panto this year, we wanted to stay at home for a change and we had enough work around the Midlands without going away. On the morning of 25th January 1976, I had a vasectomy (the snip). I always say the barmaid behind the bar did it with a Black and Decker, it usually gets a laugh. Having had it done they gave me a scrotum bag, from the front it looked like I was trawling for mackerel and from the back it looked as though I'd caught some. The same night I was working with Larry Grayson and when Larry came on stage he gave me some welly, I was a big part of his act that night. He told the audience things like, 'Our drummer has had the snip, he's as common as muck. He was telling me he feels as limp has a vicar's handshake.' It was all in good fun.

The following day we were back in rehearsals for Stars in Your Eyes in readiness for a twelve-week tour. Once again, we were travelling up and down the country. At the end of the twelve weeks a few of us out of the show were sent to Erdington High Street and Broad Street in Birmingham to the Allied Carpets Shops to record a TV advert. My part was to be a salesman running my hand over a carpet whilst selling it to a young lady. You couldn't hear me on the advert but I

Me, Larry Grayson and Chez McRae.

said to her, 'This would take the skin off your knees.' Anybody watching the advert and could lip read would say, did you just see what he said?

One of the venues we used to work at was the Fir Tree Restaurant in Wellingborough and Bernard Parr had booked Sacha Distel to appear there. I had a night off, so I went to see him. Sacha had his own band and I was talking to his drummer who had a ride cymbal that was 20 inches in diameter made from a circular saw with the cutting teeth ground off, the amazing thing was it sounded great. Sacha had hits with *The Good Life* and *Raindrops Keep Falling On My Head*, he was also a terrific guitarist and in his time he had played guitar for Lionel Hampton and other well-known bands. With our agent staging the show, I was able to get backstage and meet Sacha and chat to him about his jazz playing days, he told me he had played guitar for Dizzy Gillespie and Tony Bennett. He spoke excellent English and he was very charming, the ladies loved him.

Gerry and the Pacemakers was our next show and guess what? We were on our travels yet again back down to the south of England and on our return home we were working with Frank Ifield. Frank was born in England but his parents were Australian, he had hits with *Confessing* and *I'll Remember You* to name a few. We were towing the caravan from club to club and Frank would drop in to the caravan where Eileen would make him a cup of tea and a sandwich before we went to work in the club, he was a nice chap.

One Sunday we did an afternoon gig in Hereford, after the show Billy and I had to stay behind to rehearse our next week's act. Clive Brandy turned up with none other than P.J. Proby the American singer, dressed in his cowboy boots and stetson hat. Proby had hits with *Somewhere, Maria* and *Hold Me*. His real name was James Smith and I took an instant dislike to him from the start. Within five minutes of the rehearsal, Proby had insulted Billy's keyboard playing, which Billy didn't deserve, so he walked away from the rehearsal and told Proby to get somebody else to play for him. I didn't blame Bill at all.

We were due to play for Proby that night in Coventry, so Clive went off after Billy and talked him in to coming back. We finished

Frank Ifield.

the rehearsal then packed the gear, raced from Hereford to Coventry and just about made it in time. The venue was packed out and in the audience were an act I had played with a few times, the Krankies, Janette and Ian who were living in Coventry at that time. We played the first half of the show and then it was time for top of the bill, the act everyone had come to see, P.J. Proby. He came on stage in his Elvis Presley style clothes, he told everybody that the shirt he was wearing was given to him by Elvis Presley. But he didn't go down very well with the audience, they seemed disappointed in him, in fact if I remember correctly someone was flicking beer mats at him. After the show we were having a drink in the lounge and Proby had a lady with him and also a little girl around six or seven years of age, Proby was using bad language in front of this little girl, which I didn't think was right. Suddenly he fell on the floor spark out, after a short time he sort of came round. I don't know if he was on something or if it was the drink, he did drink a lot.

The rest of the week with him was a bit of a nightmare. One night in Birmingham, Proby came on stage and after a couple of songs he insulted a man in the audience. This chap jumped up and ran to the stage to punch Proby, luckily it was a very high stage and this angry man couldn't reach him. Proby ran off stage and locked himself in the dressing room. Well, you can imagine what happened, people had paid their money to see Proby and he had only sung a couple of songs then run off. To cut a long story short Bernard Parr had to promise to put on a free show at a later date. Clive Brandy would pick him up from the Arden Hotel by Birmingham Airport to take him to wherever we were working. Half the time Proby was not ready and Clive was getting fed up with him. Proby told Billy and I that if we ever got a gig that needed a singer, he would sing with us under a false name. As far as we were concerned there was no chance of that ever happening.

Our last show of the week was back at Hereford and at the end of the night Clive asked me if I would give Proby, his lady and the little girl a lift back to the Arden Hotel. I agreed and Clive said to Proby, 'You give Mike some petrol money.' I dropped him off and he gave me £5 (which in 1976 was worth about £35 in today's money). I said goodbye and drove away singing my head off because I did not have to play for him again and I promised myself that I never would. I once read that some other musicians had trouble with him as well. He now lives in Worcester so he has settled in England.

A few weeks later we went back to the club that Proby had upset, with the free show that Bernard Parr had promised. This time the so-called star was Lynne Perrie, who played the part of Ivy Tilsley in *Coronation Street*. She did a lot of singing and telling stories, she was easy enough to play for. It was plain to see that she had taken a few drinks before the show and it was a shame because I bet she was a good singer in her time.

The next few weeks were spent working with different acts such as Bert Weedon, Frank Carson and Jim Bowen. Jim was a schoolteacher who went into comedy and became a first-class comic, he also presented TV's *Bulls Eye.* Jim liked jazz and was quite a good jazz player, he played trumpet in his act and I enjoyed playing for Jim, he was an okay guy.

We were then back with the Kaye Sisters and Jim Davidson. We spent two whole days in the Hollick and Taylor recording studios making a long playing record of Stars in Your Eyes, The Golden Olden Days and Clubland Follies. We recorded extracts from each show and sold the records every night during the show. The record turned out to be quite successful and we sold a tremendous amount. Years later I found one in a charity shop, so I bought it.

Back again rehearsing a new edition of Clubland Follies for a nine-week tour, once again up and down the country. Followed by a further six weeks in Stars in Your Eyes. While we were working in the North East we travelled from Billingham across the Pennine mountains to the 99 Club in Barrow in Furness for a one-nighter. It was December and there was snow on the ground. I left my car in Billingham and hitched a lift with the Road Manager in a big van which carried the keyboards, my drums, the lighting, scenery, costumes and our dancing girls. I sat in the back with the dancers.

I remember the 99 Club's dance floor was like glass that lit up with underfloor lighting, it was quite impressive. During the evening I only had two drinks and by the end of the night I was drunk, so much so that our Road Manager had to pack my drums away. I'm sure someone had spiked my drink and it would not have been any of our gang knowing I had to play for the show. I'm convinced it had to be someone from the audience, why I've no idea, fortunately I was able to just about finish the show before I was incapable.

On our way back in the van, I lay across the dancers' laps spark out. Halfway across the Pennine mountains I came round, with one of the dancers stroking my head. The first thing I wanted to know was where were my drums? Our roadie assured me he had packed all my drums and everything was okay, but I still made him stop in the middle of nowhere in the snow and open up the back of the van so I could check. The roadie had done a good job, bless him.

We finished the tour which brought us up to Christmas and once again we decided to stay at home, it was nice to be with the family for a change. We had plenty of work around the Midlands and by the end of January 1977 it was time to rehearse the new edition of Stars in Your Eyes and then start another ten weeks on the road. Having completed the ten weeks, we were into a new show and as 1977 was the Queen's Silver Jubilee Year, Bernard Parr devised a show called Jubilee Jamboree. We took this show on the road for another ten weeks, which included Southern Ireland, where we spent a week. On the show was a comedian by the name of Steve Ford who was an Irishman who lived in Birmingham and had done for many years. When we were in Ireland I took my car and Steve travelled with me. Also on the show was a lady called Penny Nicholls who at one time sang with Henry Hall, a band leader on the BBC Radio right up to the 1960s. Penny toured Australia with The Black and White Minstrels, she was a good act, very experienced but the trouble was she liked a drink, in fact she liked a drink a bit too much.

Our first night was at Portmarnock Country Club just north of Dublin and while we were there, Steve took me to see his sister-in-law who lived in Dublin. She cooked us a breakfast with white pudding, I had never seen it before, it's the same as Black Pudding but white. We also played at Ballybunion on the Atlantic Coast, we arrived there in the afternoon and set up all the gear. We asked the chap who seemed to be in charge of things, what time did he want us to start the show? He said after the donkey derby, so go and have a drink.

We went across the car park to a pub, it was a typical Irish pub with an Irish Band playing and it had a great atmosphere. I drank the Guinness because it was beautiful, our guys and gals asked me what it was like, I told them you either like it or you don't, you have to try it for yourselves. So with that, some of them ordered Guinness and after our drink we went back to the ballroom, once again we asked when did he want us to start? Once again he said after the donkey derby, go and have a drink. So back to the pub and a drop more Guinness. After our drink we went back again for the second time, as we were crossing the car park there was a chap on a donkey, we asked him if the donkey derby had finished, he said, 'Bejeezus, I'm looking for the start.'

Eventually we got the show going. Well, the opening was a shambles, the dancers couldn't get their legs to work properly. One of the tunes in the opening was *Alexander's Ragtime Band* and when we got to the part where the words are *'They can play a trumpet call like you never heard before'*, one of the acts in the show was supposed to play the same phrase, he blew his trumpet and the fell on the floor. This was all the effect of the Guinness, there were only a few of us who you could say were okay. We managed to get to the interval and the first thing on the agenda was black coffee. The audience thought it was hilarious, these English folk drunk on our Guinness. The second half was a lot better and we ended up having a good night.

I mentioned that Penny Nicholls liked a drink, so much so she would sit in the dressing room with a bottle of brandy and the top of a hairspray can, which acted as a cup. She would keep topping the cup up with brandy and knocking it back, it was obvious she had a drink problem, such a shame because when she was on stage she was great. We were somewhere around Killarney when Penny threw a wobbly, she used to travel with the roadie and the dancing girls but for some reason she had fallen out with them and refused to go in the van. In fact, she had fallen out with most of the cast, it was the drink that was causing the problem.

The Company Manager phoned our agent in Birmingham and told him we were having trouble with Penny. He said pay her off and send her home. Well, the only people she would talk to was Steve Ford and me, so I was elected to drive her to Dublin Airport which was 200 miles away. Steve Ford sat in the back of the car with Penny, she had a bottle of brandy and a hairspray top, drinking all the way to Dublin which was about a three-hour drive. Steve had a job, sitting in the back with her trying to console her and trying prop her up. On our arrival at the airport, we had to get her a ticket to Manchester, then she wouldn't go on the plane unless I went with her. So I had to explain the situation to one of the air hostesses and she allowed me on the plane, I was surprised to be honest. Once I got her inside, I fastened her safety belt but then she didn't want me to leave and people were getting on the plane so I needed to get off. I used the magic word 'drink' and told her I was going to get her a drink and that did the trick. I had to fight my way off with people getting on, I said thank you to the air hostess at the door and I was off. What a relief, I could have ended up in Manchester with no ticket. That was the last time I saw her, whatever happened to her I just don't know.

We had to rearrange the show with Penny Nicholls gone and our last gig was at the Bee Hive Restaurant in Mullingar. At the back of the restaurant was a mausoleum in the shape of a Bee Hive, it was in the grounds of a Baptist Church. Apparently some chap, when he died, had wanted to be buried in a stone-built Bee Hive, which he was while sitting in a chair and his nurse was also buried with him. The Bee Hive was not that big, it was a bit like an Eskimo's Igloo.

It was time to say goodbye to Ireland and the Guinness and get the ferry back home. We had a great time in Ireland and the Irish people treated us well. When we did get back home, we had a couple of nights off which we needed after all the travelling and of course the Guinness. We had one week with Jubilee Jamboree then we went straight into summer season for seven weeks at the Lea's Pavilion Theatre in Folkestone with Stars in Your Eyes.

Once again, we took the caravan which we parked on a caravan site on top of the White Cliffs of Dover, there was no sign of Vera Lynn but we had a great view of the

English Channel. Arthur Brough, who starred in *Are You Being Served?* as Mr Grainger, staged many plays at the Lea's Pavilion Theatre for many years. The Theatre had a bar and the lady who was in charge of the bar was the daughter of Bombardier Billy Wells who was a British Heavyweight Boxing Champion and the man who banged that big gong at the start of the J. Arthur Rank movies. I got friendly with the lady and she told me that her dad had told her the gong was not a real gong, it was made out of paper and plaster and the sound of the gong was made by a very well-known percussionist of the day James Blades OBE, he struck a proper Chinese gong. James Blades taught percussion at the Royal Academy of Music and he was also responsible for the V for Victory signal during the Second World War on the radio. Anyone reading this who is old enough to remember the V for Victory signal will know it was morse code – two dots and a dash for the letter V and it was played on some kind of timpani drum. James Blades died in 1999 at the ripe old age of 97.

While we were at Folkestone, a charity football match was organised between our show biz 11 and the Folkestone Hoteliers 11. I played for the show biz 11 and we played on the Folkestone football ground, it had a grandstand where Eileen and Paul were watching the game. During the second half of the game, we changed into fancy dress for a bit of fun for the spectators. I went on as a French maid, kinky I hear you say, but it was my hairy bow-legs that turned the spectators on. The maid's dress was that tight I could hardly breathe. However, we won the game 1-0 with Billy Pearce scoring the winning goal. I was glad to get the maid's outfit off, I was getting wolf whistles from the crowd.

The end of the season came, the caravan was hitched up and we headed for home. We did a few shows a week with the Fortunes who had hits with *You've Got Your Troubles* and *Here it Comes Again*. Then it was Shag Connors and the Carrot Crunchers, what a name. They were all dressed up as West Country yokels, they were very funny. Afterwards we worked with Freddie and the Dreamers who had hits like *I'm Telling You Now* and *If You Got to Make a Fool of Somebody*. Freddie was only 5ft 3 but he had loads of energy jumping about the stage, sadly he died in 2006 aged 69.

Next was an eleven-week run of Stars in Your Eyes. In the December the BBC made a TV documentary of Stars in Your Eyes and they spent four days and four nights with us. We were filmed at the Forget Me Not Club, The East Birmingham Club, Canley Social Club in Coventry and Llay British Legion Club in North Wales. They filmed us rehearsing, partying and travelling, even stopping off at a Little Chef cafe. I don't know what the customers in the Little Chef thought, there were thirteen of us, plus the TV crew, all playing up like show biz people do when they get together.

It turned out that the TV producer went to the same school as me, Hill Boys in Mere Green, his name was John Clarke. At the end of four days and nights filming, the BBC gave us champagne to celebrate a successful filming. Out of the four days and nights, they condensed it down to two half-hour programmes to be broadcast over two weeks on BBC1. They called the programme *Have Show Will Travel* which was a very apt title. The BBC paid us good money and that was on top of our normal wages.

We had finished the run of Stars in Your Eyes which brought us up to Christmas and once again we stayed at home and worked locally. In the new year of 1978, we had a gig at Caesar's Palace in Dudley, which used to be Dudley Hippodrome. It was a show to raise money for Dudley Zoo and there were loads of stars on this gig: Billy Dainty, Steve Ford, Ronnie Hilton, Carl Wayne, Tommy Burton, Freddie and the Dreamers, Rod Hull and Emu, and Julie Rogers. We had something like an eight-piece band and Teddy Foster, who was married to Julie Rogers, was the band leader. We were worked to death that night, the only break we had was when Tommy Burton came on stage, his drummer used my drums during Tommy's act.

The New Vaudeville Band Show was our next venture, they had hits like *Winchester Cathedral* and *Finchley Central*. Then onto The Bachelors Show, Bernard Parr asked me if I could fix another five musicians up to play for The Bachelors. They had their own drummer, who used my drums, I also played but I played percussion items. At end of the night Bernard Parr came over to me and said, 'Mike, they don't like the Bass player, you will have to replace him.' All the guys I had booked were good musicians, including the Bass player. However, I had to sack him which was very embarrassing for me because I knew these chaps, I put the blame fair and square on the Bachelors. They were very polished and a good act, but to be honest I didn't like them as people.

Eric Delaney was our next gig, he was a drummer/percussionist and I had worked with him a few times before and being drummers we talked about drums, so I knew

Me and Eric Delaney.

him quite well. He was a real showman, his drums had lights inside them and lit up. Eric was very energetic, dashing across the stage playing on his timpani, xylophone and tubular bells, the sweat rolled off him. His kit consisted of two bass drums, four toms toms, various cymbals and he had enough equipment to fill Wembley Stadium, you name it, he had it, although one night I had to lend him my bass drum pedal because he had broken one of his. He had hits with *Oranges and Lemons* and *Delaney's Delight*. Eric played at The Talk of The Town, Benidorm for many years, he was quite an attraction over there. He also did summer seasons at the Tower Ballroom in Blackpool.

We were rehearsing Stars in Your Eyes and Bernard Parr had Matt Monro working at the Mackadown Pub in Tile Cross, Birmingham. After we had finished rehearsing, we went to the Mackadown to see Matt and we got in for nothing because it was a Bernard Parr Show. We went backstage before the show and Matt was there with a glass of brandy in one hand and a cigarette in the other hand. Matt was only small but he was a very friendly chap, he asked what we all did in Stars in Your Eyes. Eric Delaney was also on the show and with his band, was booked to play for Matt. When it was time for Matt Monro to grace the stage, he came on smartly dressed and he sang fantastically, his singing was so smooth, what a great voice he had. What a sad loss when he passed away and another sad loss was some years later when the Mackadown was demolished to make way for a supermarket.

Another five weeks with Stars in Your Eyes which took us up to the North East. We were working a club in Middlesbrough, when after the show a lady burst into the dressing room slightly the worse for wear with drink. She was a busty sort of lady with big boobs, in fact they were that big she could have breast-fed the whole of Middlesbrough. She was after autographs and autographs is what she got. One of our lads had got a permanent marker pen and signed the name of our male vocalist (who will remain anonymous) on her boobs, she thought this was great and went to all us lads, we all signed our vocalist's name on her boobs. She was over the moon with his name all over her boobs, it was like a badge of honour to her. There was one person who I might add was not over the moon and that was her very angry husband who came looking for our male vocalist. I think he wanted to change the shape of his face. Fortunately, our vocalist had already left the club. I think those names would take a bit of removing, being a permanent marker that put them there, she could have a case of very sore boobs.

We did a quick week with the group Paper Lace, one of their hits was *Billy Don't Be A Hero*. I was chatting to their drummer Peter Wright who had his drums at that time covered in lace doilies, then covered with a clear membrane over the doilies, a nice touch with their name being Paper Lace.

We were back with Gerry and the Pacemakers, working in Southend on Sea. Our next gig was at a mental hospital at South Ockenden on the A13. We had nowhere to stay after the gig, so the organisers told us we could stay in the dressing room for the night. Gerry and his band, me and Billy and the rest of the show spent the night in the dressing room, sleeping on the wooden benches and chairs, well it was better than nothing. Next morning everyone had gone for breakfast in the canteen and I was still dozing on a bench, when suddenly the door burst open and in came one of the inmates. This chap had a sweeping brush and he was swinging it like a sword. He was muttering something which I couldn't understand. The poor man's eyes looked a little bit on the wild side and he seemed to be coming at me as though he had something on his mind. I jumped up and I was out of that door faster than a bolt of lightning, I'm sure the poor man meant me no harm, but I was not taking any chances.

We did another week with the Fortunes then back with Freddie and the Dreamers. We then went into rehearsals for the Golden Greats show. I had spent ten years with Stars in Your Eyes and the sister shows and when we had performed 500 performances Bernard Parr gave us a trophy. I was the only one who had done all of the 500 shows.

The time came when I decided I was getting tired of all the travelling, I loved the drumming, but I was never home. So, I had a talk with Eileen and I decided to come off the road. I still had to make a living, so I suggested to Eileen that we could buy some sort of business, I was looking through a Birmingham newspaper when an advert caught my eye 'Crossroads Supermarket for sale'. Well, the fact I had worked in *Crossroads* for ten episodes had me interested. We went to see the place, it was in Tile Cross just down the road from the Mackadown Pub. The shop consisted of a greengrocery section, bread and cakes, a butcher's shop, frozen foods and wines and spirits. It had a very large stock room and upstairs was a Ladies Hairdressers, plus a two-bedroom flat. We took the bull by the horns and we bought it. We knew absolutely nothing about shopkeeping.

So now I had to tell Bernard Parr I was leaving at the end of the Golden Greats Show. Bernard was surprised but he wished me all the best. The end of the show came and I left.

Chapter 14

A NEW ADVENTURE

I was forced to hang up my drum sticks for a time while we got the shop up and running. I asked Gary Newbon MBE, the TV presenter, to do a personal appearance at the shop and it was packed out. Within the first couple of weeks of us taking over the shop, it happened to be when the BBC broadcast Part 1 of the documentary on Stars in Your Eyes that we had made six months earlier. Customers were coming into the shop and saying they had seen the programme. Then the following week they broadcast Part 2 and once again customers were coming and telling us they had seen the programme. It did the shop takings the power of good. In fact, we never looked back and within a few months we had doubled the turnover, we found it all very exciting.

It was at the shop that I first met the chap who delivered the bread and cakes, Bob Levy and his wife Wendy, I mentioned them earlier in the book. We became good friends and went out for meals quite often. Bob and I used to go to the Gate Pub in Sutton Coldfield where they did a jazz night. We had some great nights there, I got to know the drummer Pete Essex and sometimes he would get me up to play a couple of numbers. The guy who ran the band was Stan Davis who was a guitarist and I'd done a few gigs with him. It was at the Gate Pub that I first met a keyboard player, Mike Sullivan, we played on many, many gigs together and became good friends.

After a few months when we had the shop running smoothly, I got back to my drumming. I started playing with new keyboard players and bands that I had never worked with before, because I had been working in a different circle of music for many years. I was back working all the time but now locally. Then in 1981 I was in a show called Galaxy Gala Time, it was a nice little show. The keyboard player came from the North East and he was a great player. We did a week's rehearsal and come the opening night, I took Eileen and our friends Bob and Wendy Levy to see the show.

We were in the dressing room getting ready to go on stage and I was putting my suit on, when I looked up to see the keyboard player dressed in a lady's light blue blouse, tied in a bow at his midriff. He was wearing blue jeans that were so tight you could tell what religion he was, his glasses were supported by a diamante chain around his neck and he was wearing kinky boots. His crowning glory was a blue pill box hat with a veil. He was gay and he didn't hide it. When we walked out, there was an audible gasp from the audience which he loved. We started to play and he turned out to be a right showman which we had never seen in rehearsals, the audience were watching him more than the show, much to his delight. One night after the show we were having a drink when he came up to me and said, 'Mike, I'm off now. See you tomorrow night,' then he kissed me on the cheek and left. It went very quiet and everyone looked at me suspiciously, I said to the barman in the deepest voice I could muster, 'A pint of Guinness please.'

We had been working in the shop now for about four years when we were approached by a gentleman who already owned several shops and he wanted to buy ours. So, to cut a long story short, we sold it and made a nice profit. It so happened that a friend of mine, he had done a bit of drumming himself, owned a shop and wanted to sell it. His shop sold fancy goods in Shard End in Birmingham, we bought it and named the shop Bargains Galore. We completely changed it around and sold pretty well everything. It was one of those shops that sold everything you wanted: fancy goods, BMX bikes, scooters, climbing frames, slides, toys, watches, electrical items, radios, batteries, household stuff, stationery, greeting cards and even West Midland Bus Passes. You name it, we had it or could get it. We ended up with nearly 1,000 customers in our Christmas Club. We had four girls working for us, plus Eileen and I. It was a very busy, well-known shop.

In 1982 I was offered a resident job at the The Three Crowns near Walsall. It was with a quartet and playing guitar was John Crutchley, who with his lovely wife Tilly, had become good friends with Eileen and I. John was a great guitarist and a lovely bloke. I played at The Three Crowns for about five months when I was offered a residency at the Dilk Arms near Walsall, it was more nights with more money, so I took it. This is where I first met Bob Ingham who played keyboards. Bob was great chap, we had a lot of laughs together and above all he was a good player, he could read any music you wished to give him.

On New Year's Eve, 1982, the cabaret was a well-known comedian, who will remain nameless. He was booked to perform two thirty-minute spots. He came on and did his first spot but did not go down very well and at the end of his thirty-minutes he walked off stage to the sound of his own footsteps. He was supposed to go on stage later and do his second spot, but when the compere went to find him, he had vanished, he had climbed through the window and legged it.

We did two nights a week. One night we had our resident singers and if I remember rightly the other night was Free and Easy. It was the very first time I had done Free and Easy, so it was all new to me. I seem to remember Bob saying he had not done Free and Easy either until he worked at the Dilk. It was a good scene there and we had some good times. Bob and I left the Dilk in 1983 for better things, we worked together on shows all the time and were never out of work.

I had a phone call from a chap who was the resident drummer at a Warners Holiday Hotel in Crewe, I had been recommended by someone. The drummer wanted a night off so he told me what the gig paid and I told him it would have to be more money because I had to travel from Sutton Coldfield, eventually we agreed a price. He told me I could use his drums and he would leave the money in an envelope on the snare drum. When the night came for me to do the gig, I motored up to Crew and when I got there the band leader recognised me from when I was playing up in the North East in Stars in Your Eyes. It was a big room and the cabaret was The Moscow State Circus, there were no animals but they had jugglers, fire eaters, trick cyclists and contortionists. The act was scaled down and designed and to fit the Warners type venues. It was a cracking night.

One of the agents asked me to fix up a four-piece band to play for Jet Harris, who was the bass player for Cliff Richard and the Shadows. Jet had been given the sack from the Shadows because of his drinking, the drummer Tony Meeham also got sacked because of his lateness, or another way of putting it, his tardiness. Jet Harris and Tony Meeham teamed up together and had a couple of hits with *Diamonds* and *Applejack*. Although Jet was known as a bass player, he was also a good guitarist and he played guitar on the night we worked with him. The band I put together was Bob Ingham on keyboards, who I knew would do a great job, then I booked a guitar vocalist Dean Austin, who I once again knew was good and would know all Jet's tunes. I also booked a good bass player, but his name escapes me. Jet had no music but what he did do was send me a C90 tape with the tunes he was going to play, two of the tunes were the hits he had with Tony Meeham, which had drum solos in them. I copied the C90 tape and gave a tape to each one of the band so they could familiarize themselves with his act. On the day of the show, we had a rehearsal with Jet in the afternoon. He only had about six or seven numbers to cover an hour and quite honestly, he was going to be a bit short on time. After the rehearsal we all went and got some fish and chips, brought them back and ate them in the club. Jet was very chatty, telling us about his times with Cliff Richard and the Shadows and the films they had been in.

It was then time to start the show and the club was packed out. Sitting in the front row was none other than Jackie Turpin the boxer, and brother of Randolph Turpin who was World Middleweight Boxing Champion. Jackie was with his son Jackie jnr, who was also a boxer, before he turned to Wrestling. We played for the acts in the first half, then it was time for top of the bill, Jet Harris. Jet came on and performed his six numbers including his two hits, mixed with a bit of chat, so his act lasted about 30 minutes. He went off and the audience were shouting for more, so he came back on and did the two hits again *Diamonds* and *Applejack* and that was it, he had finished. The audience were once again wanting more. So, I shouted to Dean Austin, get up to the mic and do *Guitar Boogie Shuffle* and as good as gold he went up front and we all launched into *Guitar Boogie Shuffle* which calmed the audience down.

Bob and I were working all the time on shows such as the Tony Christie Show and The Clem Curtis Show. Clem was the original vocalist with the group The Foundations, their big hit was *Build Me Up Buttercup*. We also worked on the Birmingham Entertainments Council Annual Awards Shows. We were booked to play for The Ansells Brewery Talent Show which ran for a number of weeks, playing for the heats leading up to the grand final held at the Cadbury's Club in Bournville in Birmingham.

In 1985 Stan Stennett rang to ask if I would play on a show at the Roses Theatre in Tewkesbury, it was one of Stan's theatres and was where Stan's mate Eric Morecambe collapsed before sadly dying in hospital a little time later. So, I went along to Tewkesbury and met the keyboard player who I had never met before, he was a young guy who appeared to be very nervous. I think it was the first time this young chap had worked in a theatre and he felt a bit intimidated, there is a big difference between playing in a theatre and playing in a club. To be honest, he didn't play too well.

It was about this time that Bill Gore was putting his Oompah Band together. He called it Herr Schmitt and he asked me if would play drums for him. So, there I was dressed in Lederhosen, which meant my hairy legs and knees were on show to one and all. You wouldn't believe the amount of women who put their hands up my shorts, after a while I began to look forward to it. We had a lot of laughs in Bill's band. We used to finish the night with a drum solo and one night we were playing at an army camp. To close the night we did the drum solo, when I could hear the audience going wild, I thought to myself I'm doing well tonight. Then I looked up to see two of the soldiers dancing completely naked in front of the drums. Now, I know I had played for some striptease artists in my time, but this was crazy the women were going wild and I thought they were shouting for me.

At another club when it was drum solo time, I had finished the solo when a chap came up to Bill Gore and said, 'I will give you £20 if the drummer will do that again.' He must have had more money than sense, so we did it all again and afterwards Bill gave me £10 and kept £10 for himself, telling me his £10 was for acting as my agent, even though I had done all the work. That was Bill, bless him.

We were booked to play for a gentleman's birthday party, when halfway through the night's proceedings, a policewoman came in and arrested the birthday boy, handcuffed him and then proceeded to take all her clothes off. She was a strippergram, much to the band's delight. As true as I'm riding this bicycle, as you would only expect of me, I looked the other way.

Another time Bill said, 'Mike, we have got this gig for the brewery promoting their beer at The Nightingale Club in Birmingham, across the road from The Birmingham Hippodrome.' Bill then told me it was a gay club and I said, 'You've have got to be joking, no way am I going to any gay club wearing shorts.' Bill said, 'You will be okay, it's for the brewery.' Bill talked me into doing the gig and when the time came for us to appear at the club I took a pipe and tobacco, I borrowed the tobacco off my dad who was a pipe smoker, I wanted to look as macho as I could. We performed the first half and I kept a low profile. We used to do a drinking competition to promote the beer and Bill announced, 'We are going have a drinking competition and those who want to enter give their names to our drummer Mike Rubery.' I said, 'Thank you very much Bill,' he then walked away laughing his head off. So, I'm sitting at this table taking names during the interval, when a shadow cast over me, I looked up to see this person wearing a frock and trying to balance on six-inch heels, with hairy legs and a wig on his head which wasn't on straight, in fact it looked like he had got it on back to front. Then in a very gruff voice he said, 'Can I put my name on that list?' I said, 'Yes, what's your name?' He said, 'Gloria.' We ended up having a great night and nobody bothered us, I think it was my pipe and tobacco that did the trick.

Another night we did with the Oompah band was at a university and the act that was on with us was a very well-known lady comedienne. We were in the dressing room and she was sat on a chair dressed all in black, a black T-shirt and black leggings. She looked quite scruffy and she went on stage in the same clothes she arrived in. Bill Gore and I stood at the bar and watched her act and quite frankly we thought she was extremely crude. The audience were young students and call me old fashioned if you like, but to hear a female telling extremely rude jokes just did not seem right.

Frank Jones, an agent, was booking The Chilvers Coton Club in Nuneaton and offered me the job, it was six gigs a year and they were all shows. I had a few keyboard players, Billy Hunt was one of the piano players, Billy was a great guy and a great player, we did a lot of gigs together over the years. Eventually, Mike Sullivan joined me at Nuneaton. Mike Davenport, another agent took over and no disrespect to the previous agent but the shows improved, with the booking of more well-known acts such as Roy Walker, Johnnie Casson, Mick Miller and George Roper who had all appeared on *The Comedians* TV show.

Mike Sullivan and I were booked to play for Wee Willie Harris in Crewe, he was a little chubby chap, he had no music and we were expected to know everything he did. Perhaps he thought we were mind readers. He was jumping about and singing like there was no tomorrow, Mike and I did our best under the circumstances, to be honest we were not impressed with him.

I did a one nighter with Bernard Manning in Birmingham. Bernard sang a few songs during his act, we had no rehearsal but he was easy to play for, the club was packed out just to see Bernard and he didn't disappoint his fans. He was quite a good singer and before he was a comic he was a big band singer with the Oscar Rabin Band. Bernard was a very generous man and he did a lot for charity.

The first time I played at Sutton Football Club in Sutton Coldfield was in 1986. I played with Malcolm Aldridge, who was an excellent keyboard player. He was a very good reader, he could read music like reading a book and whenever he wrote music parts they were always bold and neat. Malcolm had worked for years on cruise ships such as the Canberra cruise liner. We played on a few shows at Sutton Football Club with Malcolm Vaughan and Ross McManus, it was while working on these shows that the committee, Charles Holt and Ron Cooper, asked us if we would help them start a Free and Easy on Sunday nights. Although Malcolm and I were not very experienced in Free and Easys, we did agree to give it a try. The committee said they would give us six weeks to get the Free and Easy off the ground. After about three weeks the club was full. Within a few weeks if you didn't get there by 7.30pm you wouldn't get a seat. This is where I first met two ladies, Arlene Holt and Dianne Cooper and both these ladies have been friends ever since.

Malcolm and I played a lot of shows together, places like Bedworth Civic Hall, we were also resident at Sketchley Grange in Hinckley. Our job was to play for people dining in the restaurant, then play for dancing afterwards. The owners would say to us don't play any of that jazz stuff. Bill Maynard, the actor, was a frequent visitor and most of the customers would be dressed in their dinner suits and the ladies would have on their long dresses. Bill Maynard would be wearing

Me and Malcolm Aldridge at Bedworth Civic Hall.

sandals with no socks, an open neck shirt and a sports jacket. When we had our break, we used to go into a little bar and have a drink, Bill would come in to see us, buy us a drink and ask us to play certain jazz tunes. He was a bit of a jazz fan, so what were we supposed to do? We would sneak a few of these tunes into our repertoire but play them very quietly hoping the management wouldn't notice.

It was about this time I met a trumpet player, John Smith, who asked me if I would play drums in his band, The Johnnie Sounds Band. It was a good band, John had played professionally for Joe Loss. Now between John Smith, Malcolm Aldridge, Bob Ingham, Mike Sullivan, Bill Gore and other bands I was never out of work.

On the 10th May 1989, Eileen and I had some wonderful news, we became grandparents to Michael jnr, Paul's son. When we heard about Michael I went down to the bottom of the garden and sat on a bench and cried like a baby. I've not been moved to tears very often in my life, but the news got to my emotions. Paul was 22 years old at the time and the relationship with Michael's mother didn't last and they split up. It was Eileen who kept on good terms with Michael's mother, so we were able to see Michael all the time and have him at weekends.

Before we started at Sutton Football Club, Malcolm had secured us a four-week job on a French ship with another two musicians who were friends of ours.

Our old shop Bargains Galore.

We had no choice but to honour the contract, so I hired another duo to cover for us while we were working on the ship. As I mentioned Free and Easy was relatively new to us, years ago you had the likes of Joe and Harry, who would play basically for all the beer they could drink but now you have ex-professional musicians playing for Free and Easy, due to the fact the shows they once played on have dried up. Even so we still got the odd Free and Easy singer moan at us if they thought we had not played quite right for them. How would they have got on in the old days with Joe and Harry?

Eileen and I had been running our shop for 13 years, when we were approached by a couple who wanted to buy it, so we decided to sell. We came to an agreement on the price and the deal was done, once again we made a profit. On the Saturday when we handed over the shop to the new owners, we put on drinks and food for our old customers to say thank you for their custom over the years. They came into the shop and brought us cards and gifts. The following Tuesday I went off to work on the ship.

Chapter 15

WHAT SHALL I DO NEXT?

So now I was working on a French ship called the Bretagne. It was a fairly new vessel at that time and could accommodate 2,000 passengers and 580 cars. It had two cinemas, restaurants, a resident doctor and there were shops where you could buy all sorts of things. We sailed from Portsmouth to St. Malo which took about 11 hours.

We played on the stern of the ship, the deck above was the Helicopter Deck. The room where we played was large, it was the full width of the ship and it had two bars, a dance floor, a stage and the seating went up in tiers. We were supposed to play three 45-minute spots a day. The first spot was at 12 o'clock midday, but if it was a nice sunny day the passengers would be sunning themselves on deck, so we would get ourselves a drink and join them. Our second gig of the day was late afternoon and our last gig of the day was 11pm, after the cabaret which was a magic act, where the magician's assistant got sawn in half twice nightly. We finished at 11.45pm and then the disco would take over till about 2am. We used to finish our set with yet again a drum solo, the band would walk off stage and leave me to play on my own for about 15 minutes. I used to go out front and play on the tables and beer glasses, anything that I could play on, then back to the drums. The band would wander back and we would finish off the set. Afterwards we would stand at the bar and nearly always, a Frenchman would come up to me and offer to buy me a drink. That was the cue for the band to move in and start talking to him, so he would end up buying four drinks. You wouldn't believe the amount of drinks we got this way.

As musicians we were classed as crew, so we had our meals with the crew in their canteen, they always had good food. Being a French ship, there was always two or three bottles of wine on the tables, so we rarely bought any drinks. If we did buy a drink it was very cheap. One day a week one of the shops would close for an hour, this was to allow the crew to buy anything they wanted at very cheap prices, this included us. We were buying litre bottles of whisky for £2, gin £2, rum £2, brandy was £3 and Southern Comfort was £3, 200 Benson and Hedges cigarettes £6. Cigars were cheap and so was Ladies Perfume. I had a big cardboard box full of stuff, I must have had £300 worth of gear for £25.

We became friendly with the ship's Purser, he would often come and see us play and then he would buy the band a drink. He spoke perfect English with an accent. A Purser on a ship has a very responsible job, he deals with all the stores, supplies, and all money onboard as well as the running of the ship. One afternoon he came and told us that we were heading for a Force 10 storm. We asked him if that was bad, he shrugged his shoulders and said it will be rough. Well, he was right it was rough, we had to stop playing. I had my cymbal stands wired up with coat hangers and linked to cup hooks screwed into the stage, so I removed them and put them in their case for safety. With those big ships there is more of the ship out of the water than under the water. With a Force 10 gale, the winds can be anything between 60 and 70mph and the waves between 30 and 40 feet high.

That particular night, I must admit it was rough, the worst storm I had been in. People were being sick all over the place. It was difficult to stand up without holding on to something. The other two lads in the band were both ex-marine bandsmen, they had even played on the Royal Yacht and they both had to go to the ship's doctor for some seasick pills. Malcolm and I were not sick. I've travelled on a few ships and never been sick, I guess I'm lucky. Obviously, nobody is allowed on deck, you could be washed overboard. It can be very frightening, furniture is falling about all over the place, glasses and bottles slide off the tables onto the floor. The best place to be is midship, there is less movement there. I was told by an old sailor, if you fix your eyes on something horizontal, something like a fluorescent light fitting, it keeps your brain stable and stops you being sick.

I went to the crew's mess and got a bottle of wine from the fridge and went down to our cabin, hanging onto the rails. I supped the wine and before long I got into my bunk and went to sleep, thanks to the wine. Next morning, we docked at St. Malo, we went up on deck and a lot of the deck furniture had been washed overboard.

Our cabin was down by the engine room so we got the hum of the engines, when we got back home I had to switch the vacuum cleaner on and put it under the bed to get to sleep. I had been home for a couple of weeks when I said to Eileen, that I would have to get a part-time job. I took myself off to the Job Centre, I had never been in a Job Centre in my life before. I was looking at the cards on the board, when one of them caught my eye, Canwell Hall wanted a gardener/

Ship's band.

handyman. Well, I'm certainly a handyman and I only live round the corner, you can't get handier than that. I knew Canwell Hall very well, I used to go up there when I was a kid, so I applied for the job. The next day I had a phone call from the owners, Mr and Mrs Shipley, asking me to go for an interview. I put a suit on and went to meet Mrs Shipley. I told her I was a musician and I didn't know much about gardening, I could cut lawns or cut hedges but I didn't really know one flower from another. Mrs Shipley was very polite and said, 'That's okay, I can tell you what's what and where I want the plants putting.' I then met Mr Shipley, I told him the same that I was a musician. He said, 'Would you drive the kids to school or collect them from school?' I said I could do that. They told me they would let me know, as there were other applicants. I told Eileen that I didn't think I would get the job, they needed a proper gardener.

The next day Mrs Shipley rang me to tell me I had got the job and that was the start of a very pleasant 25 years working for Mr and Mrs Shipley. After a short time they treated me like one of the family and in return I would like to think I gave them my loyalty. It turned out that Mrs Shipley's mother had been in the same class at school as Eileen's mother. Mr and Mrs Shipley and the family still keep in touch with me on a regular basis.

In 1994 I was booked for pantomime at the Red Rose Theatre in Rugeley. I eventually spent six years at the Red Rose during panto season. I used to take Eileen and our grandson Michael to see the pantos and I would take Michael backstage to meet the cast. I think it must have given him the bug, because when he grew up into a young man, he ended up performing in two or three pantos himself. Watching him on stage made me feel very proud because he did really well.

There is a story that has to been told here. At one of the pantomimes, in the front row, was a group of very posh school boys. Buttons was on stage in the ghost scene, Buttons said, 'Which way should I go kids?' And the kids shout, 'That way!' Buttons would point in the opposite direction and say, 'That way?' The kids would then say, 'No, the other way!' Then the ghost would run across the back of the stage to the opposite side. Buttons then said, 'Which way, that way?' and point to the opposite side. By now the kids are all shouting at him. One of these posh boys said to the lad next to him, 'Charles, don't bother shouting back, the man's obviously an idiot.'

In 1995 our son Paul came back from Tenerife, having been working over there for nine months. Early one Saturday morning, we were woken up by the telephone ringing, it was the Police telling us to get up and get dressed. They told us to wake Paul and tell him to get dressed and for all of us to go downstairs. The Police had blocked off the lane and nobody could get through. When we all got downstairs, we found that the Police had surrounded the cottages and in the garden were two Policemen with guns pointed at us and in the field were Police with Police dogs. They asked for Paul to come outside with his hands up. When he got outside they handcuffed him, arrested him and took him to Leicester in a Police car and locked him up.

When I went to the door I was told to put my hands up, still with these guns pointing at me. Just then my dad, who lived next door, came across the yard to collect his milk which had been delivered early that morning. The Police shouted at him to stop where he was and put his hands up. My dad being my dad said, 'What's up with you, you silly buggers? I've only come for my milk.' At that he picked up his milk and calmly walked back ignoring the Police's demands. The Police came into the house and turned it upside down searching everywhere, even Eileen's knicker drawer. When we asked what they were looking for, they told us they were looking for a gun. Needless to say, they found nothing. We had our grandson Michael staying with us for the weekend and while the Police were searching the house, we had to sit in the Police Van, Michael was only a little lad and he thought it was a game we were playing.

When we were allowed back into the house, Eileen made the Police cups of tea and they explained what it was all about. Apparently there had been a gun related robbery at the Alliance and Leicester in Leicester, it had been on TV showing the suspect. One of Paul's ex-girlfriends had seen it on TV and rung the police saying it was Paul Rubery, hence the armed police raid on us. I was a bit upset about all this because it was not Paul, he had been in Tenerife. That night I was playing on a show in Nuneaton so when the police phoned, Eileen took the call. They told Eileen that Paul was in the clear because when they looked at the photograph, they could see that the suspect was nothing like our Paul and they were going to bring him back home the next morning. The police also asked Eileen how I was, because they had seen how shocked I was, and they were concerned about me. Eileen explained that I was on a gig, but they were correct, at the end of the night I was completely drained.

As promised two Detectives brought Paul back home and they sat on our sofa having a cup of tea, laughing and joking, they had made Paul a bacon sandwich to keep him going. They told us they had been to see Paul's ex-girlfriend and they had given her a rollicking as Paul was nothing like the suspect. They also told her she had caused a lot of anxiety, as well as wasting Police time and energy. I think there were some sour grapes with this girl because Paul had broken off their relationship due to the fact she was an alcoholic.

On 19th October 1995, our good friend Martin Barry was getting married to his now wife Maralyn and they asked me if I would play for the reception after the wedding. The keyboard player was another old friend of mine Garry Booth, we had worked together many times. They were getting married in Mold near Wrexham, so away we went to the wedding on the given date. When we got to the chapel, the car parking was limited and we had to park in the street.

One of the other guests was Mike Carter who was a show biz act, he had also parked his car in front of one of these Welsh Cottages, where the front door opened onto the pavement. When we came out of the chapel to go to our cars, Mike Carter went to his car to be confronted by this very angry Welsh lady who was standing on her doorstep and in her Welsh accent she was ranting and raving. 'Boyo, my husband is a fireman and you have parked in his parking place. What about if there was a fire, Boyo, and he was called out to put the fire out...' Another guest, Jimmy Cricket the quick witted-comedian, shouted, 'Mike, tell her to go to blazes!' Well, it was so funny, needless to say it made the lady even more angry. We quickly got in our cars and hit the road as fast as we could, with the Welsh lady shaking her fist at us.

Meanwhile back at Sutton Town Football Club, we were having a great time on Sundays. Dianne Cooper started a Talent Contest and we had a lot of fun with this Contest. We had a so-called comedian who came on stage with his jacket inside out and told jokes that just didn't make sense, he was as funny as woodworm in a cripple's crutch. Then we had a Steel Band, there were loads of them in the band, then there were all these dustbins they were playing, they took up half the club. When it was their turn to perform Dianne got them to set up in the car park and the judges had to go outside to do the judging, Dianne was hoping that they didn't win. On a Sunday when we had packed away, we used to tell Dianne stories about our musical life and Dianne would be in fits of laughter with mine and Malcolm's stories, they were good times.

After a while Malcom left Sutton Football Club to go back to working on the ships full-time. So, I got Mike Sullivan to take over from Malcolm. Mike did the gig for some time before he left to do other things. Then I got Steve Morgan, who was another good player, Steve stayed with me for the rest of our time at Sutton Football Club until different people took the club over and it was not the same after that. So, Steve and I went to Walmley Social in Sutton Coldfield.

During 1997 my dad was not doing too good health wise, he was struggling to get upstairs. When I came home after a gig, I would go next door and get Dad on my back, I would grab the stair rail and pull us both up the stairs. I did this for a while and it was hard going, in the end we put a single bed downstairs for him. Mr and Mrs Shipley lent me a wheelchair so I could wheel Dad up the lane to give him a break from being in his house. The Hospital rang us to say they had got a bed for him, so I took Dad into Good Hope Hospital, not realising he would not come out again. The next day Eileen and I went to see Dad, the consultant in charge told us that they had x-rayed my dad and found he had lesions on his chest as big as 50 pence pieces. These lesions had travelled from his bowel to his chest, the thing was, he had bowel cancer and the consultant told us he had about ten days to live. Well, I can tell you I didn't see that coming. I was so upset, Eileen took me to the end of the corridor where I cried, I just couldn't hold back the tears. There was no way I could have gone back to see Dad, he would have known there was something wrong.

We never told him he had only a few days to live, whether he knew in his own mind I just don't know. I used to go and see him twice a day. In the bed opposite was Jeff Astle, the West Bromwich Footballer, who was suffering with a brain injury due to heading an old-fashioned leather football. Dad's legs started to fill up with water and they were leaking on the floor, Dad slipped on the wet floor and broke his femur. They put him on a morphine drip to control the pain and they put him in a room of his own. One of the last conversations I had with him, he said, 'Don't you get worrying about me.' I said, 'We all worry about you Dad, because we love you.' And I'm so glad I told him that we all loved him. He lasted about 14 days, then the hospital rang us to say my dear old dad had just passed away.

It was a bit of a blow even though we were expecting it. I was very close to my dad and I know it sounds silly but I suddenly felt like an orphan. My mother was heartbroken, so we were doing our best to console her. Having no brothers or sisters it fell on my shoulders to organise things, I don't know what I would have done without Eileen, she was great. I remember discussing the funeral with Eileen and what music we should have, she said, 'You know what your dad would have liked.' I said, 'What's that?' She said, 'You, playing something in one of the bands.' I don't know what it was but once again I burst into tears, it was the thought of playing for my dad one last time. One of his favourite tunes was *In The Mood* and it so happened I had a recording of me playing *In The Mood* with the Fred Newey Big Band, so we played it on entering the Crematory.

My mother was trying to decide which flowers we should have, she suggested we have his name in flowers, as I mentioned earlier everybody called my dad SOS Rubery. But I said it would look a bit strange, a Funeral car driving along the road with SOS on the side of the hearse. When we all got into the funeral car and drove along our lane, the tears came again and through the service in the crematorium the floor was wet with my tears.

On a lighter note, our son Paul got married for the second time, I think he was getting addicted to wedding cake. On 18th November 1999 our second grandson, Zac, was born. Zac was diagnosed as autistic, as I write this Zac has just celebrated his 21st birthday and he has grown up into a lovely young man, his pride and joy is his computer. He has proved to be a very clever chap, so much so we have nicknamed him The Awesome One, much to Zac's amusement. He keeps in touch with his brother Michael, who is another wizard on computers.

On 22nd April 1998 Mike Sullivan and I started playing at the Hill Social Club, later to become affectionately known as The Cabbage Patch, because Hill Social was an Allotments Club. We were playing Free and Easy here for some time when Mike Sullivan left to do other things. So, I asked Bob Ingham to join me and he's been with me ever since. I've had several comperes over the years, the guy who I have now is a chap I've known for a long time, Graham Payne. Graham always does a great job. So far, I've spent 22 years playing at Hill Social and I've had some great times and have made some lovely friends there.

On 8th May 2001, Paul and his wife Keri gave us another grandchild, this time a granddaughter, Kelsey. Kelsey contracted Dermatomyositis also known as JDM, a very rare disease and she was in the Birmingham Children's Hospital for quite a while. Paul would stay with her during the night, then Keri would take over in the day. We were all very worried about Kelsey but she pulled through and is now 19 years of age and at this time of writing, she is studying Health Care.

John Smith, Mark Champion and I ran a band, later known as the Alpha One Swing Band. I eventually put this band on at Hill Social Club once a month. We were forced to sack the original piano player and singer due to bad behaviour, so we had to find replacements. Taking over the vocalist job was Clint Hill and the gentleman who came and played piano for us was Ken Ashby. When Ken came into the band it made a big difference, not only was he a first-class piano player, he could also play trumpet and he could sing as well. The icing on the cake was, he could write band arrangements and as the years have gone by, Ken has supplied the band with band arrangements on a regular basis, in fact Ken has become irreplaceable.

We do have a couple of guest singers come and perform with us every so often. One is Paul Drakeley from the Rat Pack and the other one is Ken Ashby's daughter Collette, who has a great voice and a lovely personality. Clint Hill, our main vocalist, works hard bringing new songs to the band, he's got a large range of numbers from swing to rock and roll, he also plays the harmonica. All this is with the help of Ken Ashby writing the arrangements for him.

Other regular members of the band I've not mentioned are Sharron Brown who plays saxophone, she and I have worked together many times in smaller bands and I can honestly say her playing is terrific. Then there is Paul Hughes, another well-known saxophone player, he always gives a hundred percent to any band he plays in and I would recommend him to any band leader. On trombone is a chap who has been with us for a long time, that is 'Woody' Woodward, a real character who plays a hot trombone. He doesn't hold back and he is another musician who always gives you a hundred percent, plus Woody has a great sense of humour, which makes for a happy band. Our bass player is the youngest, although I have mentioned him, I feel I should tell you a bit more about him. Mark Champion is a really nice chap, he and I get on well together. I know Mark won't mind me saying this, he has not had the experience that the rest of us have had yet but you wouldn't know it. I know when I have got Mark odd jobs playing in big bands, he gets nervous and I tell him there is no need to be. Whatever music you put in front of Mark he reads it and plays it, he has a natural feel for his Bass playing and he gets a nice sound from his Bass, he's another one I would recommend to any band leader.

In 2004 I started playing for Frank Partridge at Bournville in Birmingham, at a jazz night run by Jim Denham, a great character who also plays the drums and sings. Having said that, Jim is a mine of information on jazz, we have had many conversations concerning jazz and have exchanged many jazz stories with each other. Jim is a well-known guy among the Traditional and Dixieland bands. I first met Frank Partridge in the 1960s and he is a great piano player, I've always held Frank's playing in high regard. Our saxophonist at Bournville is Dave Rushton, yet another good jazz player. The Bass player is Tony Sharp who never seems to be out of work, which tells you one thing, he's a good player. We play at Bournville once a month and we get visiting musicians who get up and jam with us, which makes for some great nights.

A gig Bill Gore and I were asked to do was for Cadbury's at the International Convention Centre, next to the Symphony Hall in Birmingham. Cadbury's had asked our agent for two people to be the Cadbury's Cow, Esmeralda. So, Bernard sent Bill and I, we had been given a cow costume a week before the gig so we could practise walking in it. We tossed a coin to see who was going in front and who was going in the back end, I lost the toss so I was the rear end of the cow. So, there we were in the field at the side of my cottage practising, I was in the back end bent over, hanging on to Bill's belt. While we were in the field I noticed a big black bull grazing and eyeing us up suspiciously. When we started walking like a cow, this big black bull looked up and started galloping like mad towards us. I said, 'Bill, that black bull is coming after us what are we going to do?' Bill said, 'I'm going to chew grass, you had better brace yourself!'

When the day came for us to go and do our interpretation of a Cadbury's Cow we got to the ICC in the morning, ready for rehearsals, the ICC is a big theatre type of a place with a massive stage. When the compere introduced Esmeralda the Cadbury's Cow, we were supposed to then trot on to the sound of a very loud 'Moo!' Jill Dando from TV's *Crimewatch* was also on the show and it was her job to milk Esmeralda into a large stainless steel bucket. Having milked the cow, she would put her hand into the bucket and pull out a sign that read 'A glass and a half of milk in every bar' and that was the gist of it.

Having done the rehearsal, we had a break when they gave us coffee and sandwiches, we chatted to Jill Dando, she was very nice to us and she was a very attractive lady. After the break, the audience were coming in and the place was full, it was to promote Cadbury's Chocolate so there was more to it than just us being milked. At the back of the stage was a massive screen showing the new TV advert for that upcoming Christmas and telling the story of Cadbury's. When it came for us to make our entrance, we trotted on stage, once again to the sound of a loud 'Moo!' Jill Dando sat on a three-legged stool and milked us, with me bent over and Jill sitting on the stool, our heads were close together but of course no one could see me. While Jill was milking us I said, 'Jill, be gentle with me, my udder is a bit tender,' and poor Jill started laughing, thank goodness the audience couldn't hear us.

Esmeralda, Cadbury's cow.

On the side of the stage was a pallet load of Cadbury's chocolates, everything that Cadbury's made. The guy in charge told us to help ourselves, so I found a cardboard box and I filled it up with all sorts of their chocolates and took them home. There was enough chocolate to last us six months. Tragically, it was about two years later that someone unknown shot Jill in the head on her own doorstep. She was a lovely lady and she didn't deserve what happened to her.

I did a couple of spells on the Ivy Benson all girl band show. We played for the first half of the show then Ivy and her 15-piece band did the whole second half. I thought it was a great band, much underrated and a lot better than people gave it credit for. I used to chat to her drummer Crissy Lee, she was quite a good drummer. Ivy Benson was originally a saxophone player but she ended up playing piano with her band.

Another band I played for was called The Eureka Jazz Band, a New Orleans type of band run by a trombone player, Terry McGrath. We did a lot of gigs where we would saunter along playing jazz like they do in New Orleans. I had to play all the jazz on a snare drum that was attached to my belt and all this was new to me, but I soon got into the swing of things. We played at Coombe Abbey and guest of honour was Barbara Windsor. She arrived in the film star car Chitty Chitty Bang Bang. We had to surround the car and play *Chitty Chitty Bang Bang*, then Barbara stood up and waved to the crowd.

It was while I was working with Terry McGrath and The Eureka Band that we played in front of 22,000 people, the biggest audience I had ever played in front of and that was at the Edgbaston Cricket Ground. It was a test match and when the cricketers had their lunch and tea breaks we played on the pitch to entertain the crowd.

Another one of these gigs we did was at an Asian wedding. We started off playing at the Tower Ballroom in Birmingham, we came out of there and we ambled down the road playing all the jazz tunes, directly behind us was the bridegroom who was mounted on a large white horse, a real horse I might add. The bridegroom also had a big sabre attached to his waist and his clothes and head gear were amazing, very colourful, it was a fantastic sight. There were loads of Asian people walking along with us dressed in their traditional clothes and as we were playing along the road these Asian people were coming up to us and giving us money. The only one of us who had a free hand was the bass drummer Andy Lowe and he was the one they were giving the money to. As we were progressing along the Hagley Road in Birmingham the police were having to direct the traffic around us. When we got to the Clarendon Suite where the wedding was being held, which at that time was a Masonic Lodge, we formed a guard of honour and played as the guests went into the Clarendon. When it was time for Terry McGrath to pay the musicians their wages, the money that the people gave us was split up between us, so we had an extra bit of money for our efforts.

We also played at Drayton Manor when Noel Edmonds opened the new Water Splash Ride. We escorted him to the Water Splash, as we played he walked between me and the bass drum player, people were lined up along the road to see him, he waved to the crowd as we progressed along the road. I played quite a few of these type of gigs with Terry McGrath.

We were on the Vince Eager Show when also on the show was The Mighty Atom and Roy, The Mighty Atom later became Big Mo who ran the Roly Polys with Les Dawson. The Mighty Atom was on the first half of the show and the second half was left to Vince Eager. Vince had been on stage for a short while, when an argument started between two guys in the audience it soon got out of hand and the one chap broke a glass and jammed it into the face of the other chap. Well, women were screaming and there was blood all over the place, it was not nice and no one was taking any notice of the show, they were getting up and leaving. Vince just stopped singing and in his frustration, threw his guitar on the floor and walked off stage, so that was the end of that show.

It was at this time I was invited to join the The British Nuclear Test Veterans Association (BNTVA). The chairman of the West Midlands branch was a Scotsman, Archie Hamilton Ross. Archie worked tirelessly for the veterans, as both Archie and his daughter were affected, more so his daughter, she suffered quite badly. Over the years Eileen and I became good friends with Archie and his wife Chris. The aim of the BNTVA was to get compensation for us nuclear veterans, a lot of us have suffered with health problems due to our exposure to radiation, also a lot of our children and grandchildren have been affected. We held our meetings each month at the Nautical Club in Birmingham. We also had many Birthday and Christmas parties and I used to take different bands and play for these parties. At one time the Association ran out of money, so I arranged a couple of shows to raise some funds and the Association presented me with a Crystal Beer Glass engraved with my name and some kind words, it's one of my treasured possessions. We became a close-knit bunch of ex-servicemen from the Army, Navy and RAF but sadly, over the years most of our veterans have passed away.

The Ministry of Defence still refuse to accept the fact that some of our veterans have suffered. I, myself, seem to be okay (but my piles do light-up in the dark). Joking apart, my three grandchildren have all had health problems, whether their problems have been caused through me being sent to Christmas Island (now called Kiritimati) is hard to prove. It's not a very nice feeling to think I might be the reason why my grandchildren have had health problems. Other countries, such as the USA, automatically compensated their veterans.

I had met a guy who was to become one of my best friends, he is a guy who has a lot of talent, he started playing drums as a young man in his dad's band. Eventually he hung up his drum sticks and became a great vocalist performing on TV with his own dancing girls. After becoming a first-class vocalist, in turn he became a comedian, so now he's classed as a vocalist/comedian. He has worked with top names such as Antony Newley and he's a man with a warm personality. The man I'm referring to is my pal, J.P. James. Over the years we have worked together on many, many shows. J.P. James has produced several Production Shows of his own, on which I've been privileged to play drums and we have had a lot of fun.

We were playing at the Prince of Wales Theatre in Cannock when one of the dancing girls pretended to be a crazy wardrobe mistress, who had an overwhelming urge to sing a song on the show. The idea being, she would come on stage dressed in her overalls and wearing these short-sighted glasses, looking like a nerd. She would interrupt J.P. and plead with him to let her sing, at the same time she would hang on to his trousers. J.P. would say, 'Elsie, you can't sing. Your job is backstage, wardrobe and props.' J.P. then said, 'Get off the stage and get back to your job.' So, she goes off stage with her head bent all disappointed and the audience would all go, 'Ahhhh! Let her sing.' This routine went on throughout the show, when at last she came on stage pleading with J.P. to let her sing and still hanging on to J.P.'s trousers. The idea was, Elsie would snatch J.P.'s trousers off, which were velcroed together, thus leaving J.P. standing there in his boxer shorts.

Now this had worked okay on previous shows, but on one particular night when Elsie grabbed his trousers, she didn't realise she had grabbed his boxer shorts as well. She yanked the trousers and down they came along with his boxer shorts, so poor J.P. stood there with his meat and two veg on view in front of 400 people. He immediately tried to cover himself up with his hand, I was in the orchestra pit and had a hand towel I used to mop my face, so I shouted up to J.P. and threw him the towel. He had a microphone in his left hand and instinctively he caught the towel in his right hand, thus once again putting his crown jewels on display yet again. The theatre audience were in uproar, laughing their heads off. J.P.'s wife was in the audience and she said after, 'I was glad when you covered things up.' He asked, 'Why?' She said, 'Well people will think I married you for your money.'

Hi there, it's me again, J.P. James. Here's a story that sums up Mike Rubery's sense of humour. Swing Masters Tony Hooper on keyboards and Rob Evans on Bass and myself and Mike Rubery were doing a Rat Pack Swing gig at this very posh wedding. We arrived early to set up our equipment and whilst the wedding party were having their meal and speeches etc, we were in a covered porch area outside having a cup of tea. We were joined by two young chaps who were waiters, also having a break. These two chaps both lit cigarettes and as we were non-smokers we were concerned for their health, I pointed out to them that there were 57 different chemicals in cigarettes to keep people addicted and the damage to your lungs would be permanent. These two chaps were totally unimpressed and carried on smoking. Then Mike took over the sermon. Mike told them how his dad would light up a cigarette and when he had smoked that one would light a new cigarette with the nub end of the old one, it's called chain smoking. He would then throw the nub end on the floor and grind it out with his foot, until there was nothing left but dust, he would do this 20 times a day. Mike's face was tortured, he was so intense that we were all hypnotized by him. Mike then said, 'It got him in the end, my dad died,' he paused. 'He died of cancer of the foot.' Well, we laughed till we cried, the two chaps just gave a look of total confusion and walked away in silence, which made it even funnier! Nice one, Mike. (J.P. James)

Thanks J.P., I do remember that incident with those two lads and you guys laughing. J.P. I also had an uncle who drank a lot, in the end he started to get the shakes which caused him to spill his drink all over his shoes, he sadly died of cirrhosis of the shoelaces!

There are a few funny stories. I remember playing in that big Hotel in Stratford-on-Avon, it used to be the Hilton Hotel. The Swing Masters were booked to play for a very large party of builders, in fact they were roofers. Well dear reader, to put it bluntly we died on our arses, we couldn't do anything right for this lot. Poor J.P., we could only feel sorry for him, these roofers were just not interested in anything he did, I think the problem was they were drinking Night Nurse. Well, the roof fell in on us that night. If any act or musician tells you they have never died on their backside, then they are telling lies. Anyone who has been in the game for a long time, I said in the game not on the game, sooner or later it will happen to you. J.P. and I still laugh about the roofers gig.

Another thing that can happen to you in clubs is what they call, getting paid off. If you have not gone down very well with the audience in the first half the Entertainments Secretary will, during the interval, give you half your wages and tell you you're not needed for the second half. I was once told that this could be a bit of a fiddle, they give you half your money and pocket the other half for themselves. How true that is I don't know. However, there have been acts that have definitely needed to be paid off.

A keyboard player from Leicester once asked me if I would go to Germany for a one nighter with him, to play at a British Army Barracks in a place called Bunde, in Lower Saxony. It was about 30 miles from Osnabruck, where I was stationed in 1958. We travelled in the keyboard player's car, with drums and keyboards. We drove down to Dover and caught a ferry to Zeebrugge in Belgium. We drove across country into Osnabruck in Germany, where we stopped outside the Barrack Gates were I was stationed, then carrying on to Bunde, which was about a five-hour drive from Zeebrugge. We arrived at the venue and set up our gear in the NCOs' Mess, they gave us something to eat and afterwards we had a sleep in one of the prisoners cells in the guard room, until it was time for us to get ready to go on stage.

Now this keyboard player was a good player and he also sang, he was a pro-musician. When we started we could see there was only a handful of people in the room but we played the amount of time we were asked to do. When we came off stage, this mouthy corporal came up to us and said we were rubbish and he didn't want to pay us. Well, the keyboard player was so distraught and upset, he phoned the agent and explained the situation. It was plain to see what the trouble was, this corporal had also got a Disco booked who was a German from Osnabruck, who he used on a regular basis and he didn't want to upset him. Because there were not many people in, he was losing money and we were the easy option to pay off, or in our case, not to pay at all. The mouthy corporal ended up out of pocket, the agent made him pay our full money, knowing the keyboard player was not rubbish. The embarrassing thing was packing away our gear in front of what audience there was.

We loaded up the car and made our way back to England. We travelled through the night and the piano player could not come to terms with what had happened. We had to get home as quick as we could, because we were playing at Coventry Railway Club the next night, where we had a great night which restored the keyboard player's confidence. It was a long way to go, 600 miles, to get paid off, but we did get paid our full money much to the mouthy corporal's cost.

I got the Alpha One Band a gig at Stoneleigh Abbey, where we played all 1940s music. We had purchased a set of 1940s American Army Uniforms, so we looked

J.P. JAMES AND THE SWING MASTERS

Mike Rubery   Tony Hooper   Rob Evans   J.P. James

Mark Betts, J.P. James and myself.

the part and we were there for two days. They asked me if I could put a band on the following year, this time it was at Kelmarsh Hall, and the theme was the History of Music so I got the Swing Masters the gig. Being the History of Music, the music ranged from medieval times up to the modern-day music, we were asked to perform the swing era. Terry Jones from *Monty Python* performed the medieval period. We did the gig with original Swing Masters, who were J.P. James, Tony Hooper, Rob Evans and me. Once again, we were booked for two days.

The present line up of the Swing Masters consists of just three of us J.P. James, Mark Bettis and me. When J.P. James and I first met Mark, he was a teenager and but even then he was a brilliant keyboard player, as the years have gone by Mark has developed into a first-class player and has been part of the Swing Masters now for many years.

Ken Ashby asked me to play in a band that he ran at the Forest Arts Centre in Walsall, it was a Jazz Workshop. Once again Ken put his expertise to good use by writing new arrangements for us to play, I found it very useful to be able to hone my reading skills. Drummers don't get the chance to keep up with their reading, unless they play in a big band. I'm lucky playing in several big bands, I am able to keep on top of the reading. I knew all the musicians at the Jazz Workshop which was nice, the Bass player was a good friend of mine, John Griffiths. John is good player and we have worked on many gigs together in different bands.

Chapter 16

NOTHING LASTS FOREVER

In 2009 my mom started to feel unwell, complaining of a fuzzy head and after a while it was clear there was something wrong. We couldn't get her to come downstairs, when we asked her to come down she would say, 'In a minute.' The doctor told us that it was dementia and we would have to do the best we could. When my dad passed away, I had made a doorway between the two cottages so she could come through to us anytime she wanted. Eileen would do the cooking and Mom would have her meals with us. In the end we had to bring her bed downstairs, where we could keep an eye on her. However, things got worse and she started to fit, which we could not understand because she had never had fits in her life before. Eileen immediately phoned for an Ambulance and they arrived very quickly. Mom was still having a fit and the medics were working on her trying to stabilize her condition.

When they got her to Good Hope Hospital, they scanned Mom's head and found she had a brain tumour. The consultant showed me a picture of the tumour and it was the size of my fist. He told me that he had been in contact with the surgeon at the Queen Elizabeth Hospital in Birmingham and they had told him because of her age there was nothing they could do. In fact, she wouldn't survive the operation due to her age, she was just short of 96 years of age. A couple of days later the hospital phoned to say my mom had passed away. Mom's youngest sister, my Aunty Elsie, had come to stay with us at this time and all three of us went straight to the hospital to see her. When I looked at her it was as though she was asleep. We were all upset and more tears, but once again I don't know what I would have done without Eileen. We got through the funeral and I put my mom's ashes in with my dad's ashes, in my grandad's grave.

There are a couple of people I feel I should mention that I have known for many years, Gordon and Jan Andrews, who have been our accountants since the 1960s.

Since then, we have become good friends and have been to many parties, nights out and meals together, sometimes with some of their well-known clients. Sadly, Gordon passed away on 12th December 2020, but I'm still in touch with Jan.

Another friend of ours is Mike Murphy who has dealt with our financial affairs for many years and also done work for my family. He has always done a first-class job and is still looking after my finances to this day. I have £350 in three different banks, when I get a bank statement it's pinned to a wreath!

Through the years up to 2012 not much happened but I was working all the time. I was playing in several big bands, as well as deputising in other big bands such as the Four Oaks Big Band and Graham Nock's Phoenix Big Band, I also played in another old friend John Ruddick's big band.

In 2013, Bill Gore fell seriously ill, so I used to go and see Bill at his home once a week. He was so weak, a single bed had to be put downstairs for him. One day when I had gone to see him, he told me there was no hope for him and that he didn't have much time left. Then he asked me if I would speak about him at his funeral and I told him I would be honoured to do so. I could feel myself filling up, but I tried not to show it. I felt sorry for his wife Christine, she had to cope with the thought of losing Bill. The inevitable happened and Bill passed away, I got together with Christine and the vicar, a very pleasant lady called Ruth Souter. Having sorted out the arrangements over the next few days I wrote six pages of A4 paper on the life and times of Bill Gore. I spoke about the time he worked on the railway, when he became a fireman on the footplate of the Flying Scotsman Steam Train, Bill at one time even fired the Royal Train. Then in his show biz days, he won *Opportunity Knocks* no less than five times.

I was asked to join a couple of big bands in Coventry, one band was called The Meridians Big Band, run by a lady called Lisa Bartley. The other band was The Westwood Big Band which was run at that time by Brian Cox. After Brian gave up the leadership, it was then taken over by a trombone player named Howard Burrows. Over a period of time I've become friends with both Brian and Howard. Brian Cox was one of the trumpet players in the band and he is a retired QC (Queen's Counsel) who became famous in 1988 due to the fact he was the very first Barrister/QC to prove someone guilty using DNA evidence. The man in question was Colin Pitchfork who had raped and murdered two young girls – 15 year old Lynda Mann and 15 year old Dawn Ashworth. Brian won the case. Another famous case Brian was involved in was the Birmingham University Small Pox case and once again Brian won the case.

I played in Brian's small band and when it was his birthday, he would celebrate by putting on a birthday bash, with his 6 or 7-piece band to entertain his family and friends. One of Brian's friends was Kenneth Clarke MP who was a jazz lover. Before the gig, Brian introduced me to Kenneth as his Brummie friend and Kenneth had a laugh at the way we brummies speak. I did notice that Kenneth liked a nice pint of beer.

In 2013 another old friend Bernard Parr, my agent, sadly passed away and his family asked me if I would speak about Bernard at the funeral, once again I said I would be honoured to do so. I wrote seven pages of A4 sheets all about Bernard. Two days before Bernard's funeral, I was cutting wood on my circular saw for our wood burner, I don't know what happened I must have let my concentration slip, but I pushed my thumb on my right hand into the circular saw. I rushed into the house and put my thumb under the cold-water tap, Eileen took one look at it, put a tea towel round it and insisted she took me to the hospital. As you would expect there was a queue of people in the A & E department. Having checked in we sat down in the waiting room, by now the pain was beginning to kick in so much so I was starting to pass out. I was trying to hang on but I was losing the battle. Eileen went to see if someone could help and within minutes a nurse came and got me, Eileen helped the nurse hold me up. They sat me down and gave me some morphine, then put me on a trolley and took me to the x-ray department. Then they brought me back to see the doctor who was a young lady, her first words were, 'And who's a silly bugger then?'

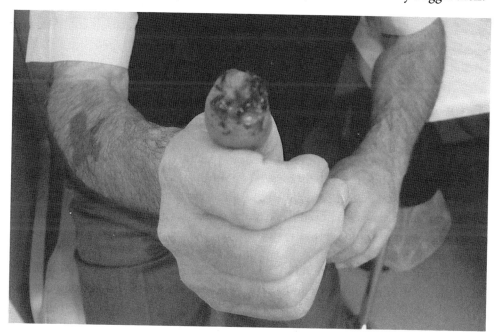

Two weeks after I cut my thumb.

I was very worried, my thumb was a mess and I kept thinking, am I going to play drums again? I told the doctor that I was worried and why, well it was like saying a magic word, she was extra careful when she injected my thumb and gently sewed me up. She was asking me questions about the music world and after she had finished she gave me some painkillers to take home, then gave me a hug and hoped my thumb got better. The x-ray showed that the circular saw had just missed the bone, I was very lucky, I could have lost half my thumb but it is a bit shorter than the other one.

So, there I was at Bernard's funeral with my right hand bandaged up like a boxing glove. To be honest I was still feeling a bit groggy, but I didn't want to let Bernard's family down. The crematorium was full and when I was called up to give my tribute to Bernard, I'm glad to say things went according to plan in spite of my injury. Glen, Bernard's wife still keeps in touch and that means a lot to me.

My hand was out of action for about four weeks and I had to get another drummer to play for me until I was able to get back to playing again. I did heal up quite quickly and after that I was very careful when I was cutting up wood. My thumb is still numb and in cold weather quite painful.

In 2018 Eileen and I, after much soul searching, decided to sell the cottages and downsize to something smaller. I said soul searching because I was born and bred in the cottages, it was going to be a big wrench for me and Eileen realised that. There was a lot of work involved with the running of the cottages, it was a big place to look after, plus the fact there was only Eileen and I living there. So, we made the decision to sell and look for a bungalow, we looked at several properties till we found one that suited us. After a lot of toing and froing we sold our cottages and we moved into our bungalow in February 2019.

Then 2019 turned into the blackest and worst time of my entire life. The first thing was my cousin Linda's husband Bill Jones passed away, then we heard that Eileen's youngest brother Geoffrey had passed away in Thailand. On 15th September, another cousin Sheila's husband passed away, he was Sir Michael Edwardes, who was at one time in charge of British Leyland in the 1970s/80s. Sir Michael sadly died of Parkinson's Disease and the last time I spoke to him was when he and Sheila came to my mother's funeral.

The 3rd October was our 55th Wedding Anniversary and Graham Payne had told me about a place called The Spotgate Inn where you could have a meal in a Pullman Railway Carriage. So, with our friends Bob and Wendy Levy, Eileen and I decided to give it a try and we ended up having a lovely afternoon sitting in a first-class carriage eating a first-class meal on our 55th Wedding Anniversary.

Four days later on 7th October 2019, three weeks after Sir Michael Edwardes had passed away, I had the biggest shock of my entire life. My dear Eileen died suddenly. At 5.15am in the morning, when Eileen got out of bed to go to bathroom, I heard a loud bump. I shouted to Eileen but there was no answer, so I leapt out of bed and went to the bathroom and to my dismay there she was on the bathroom floor. I can remember panicking and shouting, 'Eileen! Eileen!' but there was no response. I phoned 999 as quick as I could. I then phoned my son Paul and of course he was still in bed at that time of the morning. I then phoned my daughter-in-law who came round to me as quick as she could. The Medics were at our door very quickly and they worked on Eileen in the bathroom, one of the questions they asked me was, did I want Eileen resuscitated? This question hit me like a sledgehammer, I snapped back at them, 'Of course I do.' I thought what a question to ask. I didn't mean to be rude, but this was my Eileen and I didn't want her to die.

Two Ambulances turned up and they got her into one of them while still working on her. I got into the other one and we went to Good Hope Hospital. The lady driving the Ambulance I was in, told me to prepare myself because it wasn't looking good for Eileen. My family all met up at the hospital, I've not got a big family, but they were all there. We had a lady doctor who was very nice, she kept us updated as we all waited. I felt numb with the trauma of it all. In the end the doctor came and told us Eileen had passed away. They brought Eileen into a side room for us to see her, I kissed her and said goodbye. Paul and our granddaughter took Eileen's rings off her fingers and I now wear her rings on a chain around my neck. When I looked at Eileen lying there it didn't seem to be my Eileen, it was so hard to cope with. The lady doctor could see I was in a bit of a state and she put her arms around me and gave me a hug, which I thought was very kind of her.

When we got home, I just sat on the sofa in a state of shock. My family were there with me, Paul and my daughter-in-law Keri were phoning family and friends informing them of what had happened. When Keri phoned J.P. James he was on his way to Torquay for a few days break. He received the call on his mobile phone while he was at a service station on the motorway, when Keri told him what had happened, he was so upset he turned his car around and came back home. The next day he came to see me, that's what you call a good friend. I kept shaking violently, Paul put a blanket over me thinking I was cold, but it was the shock coming out. I know I'm not on my own when it comes to grieving, I know there will be people reading this that have gone through the same agony as me when they have lost a loved one. But I would like to think that me pouring my heart out might be of some help to anyone reading this who finds themself in the same position as me.

The inquest revealed that Eileen had died of Deep Vein Thrombosis. When it came to arranging the funeral, Mike Sullivan offered to play the organ at the crematorium. I was touched by Mike's offer, not only did he play the organ, but he also sorted out the music. I told him the hymns and music I had chosen and he sorted it all out with the Funeral Director, Mr Ian Hazel. Having done all this for me, after the funeral Mike took a keyboard to Hill Social to play for us after the funeral, so like J.P. James, Mike Sullivan proved to be a true friend and I won't forget that.

During the Service another friend of mine Martyn Brown read a lovely poem called *Look For Me in Rainbows* and J.P. James spoke about Eileen. Ian Hazel told me there was over 200 in attendance at the crematorium and afterwards we had a full room at the club. Mike Sullivan played keyboards while people chatted and had the buffet. The way I felt at that time was, I didn't think I would ever want to play drums again and I said as much to some of my musician friends at the funeral. Straight away they said, especially Graham Nock, that I must keep playing as it would be a life saver. And I'm glad to say I took their advice. Garry Allcock, another drummer friend of mine, very kindly played for me for a few weeks until I could get my head together and get back to playing again.

I would like to take this opportunity to say a special thank you to all my musician friends who have been so supportive through my sad time. Another good friend of mine, Bob Levy, has taken me out once a week for lunch and phones me regularly, he's been a good mate.

Now dear reader, in conclusion to my story, I will leave you with this thought. Anyone who is married or in a relationship, sooner or later one of you will have to go through the agony of losing the other because 'Nothing Lasts Forever'.

THE END